Letters *from a* PRISONER

A Story of Hope and Redemption

RACHEL JOY MCCARTHY

Healy Quinn Publishers
Portland, Oregon

RACHEL JOY MCCARTHY

HEALY QUINN
PUBLISHERS

Copyright © 2019 by Rachel Joy McCarthy

Scripture quotations marked (NIV) are taken from the Holy Bible, New International Version®, NIV®. Copyright © 1973, 1978, 1984, 2011 by Biblica, Inc.™ Used by permission of Zondervan. All rights reserved worldwide. www.zondervan.com The "NIV" and "New International Version" are trademarks registered in the United States Patent and Trademark Office by Biblica, Inc.™ New American Standard Bible® (NASB), Copyright © 1960, 1962, 1963, 1968, 1971, 1972, 1973, 1975, 1977, 1995 by The Lockman Foundation Used by permission. www.Lockman.org. (NLT) are taken from the Holy Bible, New Living Translation, copyright ©1996, 2004, 2015 by Tyndale House Foundation. Used by permission of Tyndale House Publishers, Inc., Carol Stream, Illinois 60188. All rights reserved.

For speaking engagements please contact
Speaking@KevinMcCarthy.com, or visit LettersFromaPrisoner.com.

For order or bulk purchases of this book, please write
Books@KevinMcCarthy.com.

Healy Quinn Publishers, Portland, Oregon

Edited by Kimberley W. Eley
Cover design by Chris McCarthy
Back cover photo by David Schelske

McCarthy, Rachel Joy

Letters from a prisoner: A story of hope and redemption / Rachel Joy McCarthy

ISBN: 0-9991034-4-9
ISBN-13: 978-0-9991034-4-9

Printed in the United States of America

A NOTE FROM THE AUTHOR

While my husband Kevin was incarcerated for almost three years, he wrote me letters — almost daily. Though writing letters is somewhat a thing of the past, for us it was our best means to communicate, since phone conversations were both regulated and costly and visitations were infrequent. Writing each other also had a therapeutic value to it—just knowing someone was "on the other side" waiting to receive a lifeline from their loved one made all the difference in the world.

I am not a hoarder of many things, but I am truly guilty of hoarding his many letters. Fortunately, this worked to my advantage when I decided to tell my side of the HMC/Znetix scandal and how our lives were completely turned upside down in the fray. I have used Kevin's letters, my journals (of which I am also a hoarder), snippets of news articles, and the recesses of my memory to recall this story as accurately as possible.

Most of the names you read are real people whom I dearly love that the Lord used to help me navigate this frightening, unchartered territory. A few people's names are changed to protect them and to keep their reputation intact. No matter what part the "cast members" played in the narrative, I have no ill feelings toward any of them. Yes, there will always be questions... But I have come to accept Romans 8:28a as a common theme for my life, "And we know that God causes all things to work together for good to those who love God..."(NASB)

DEDICATION

This book is dedicated to my husband Kevin to whom I look up to and greatly respect.

You are one of the heroes of this story because you wouldn't let the punches of life keep you down. And in the process, you grew strong because of them. Your iron will has certainly worked out in your favor.

ACKNOWLEDGEMENTS

Kevin: Thank you for making my life an adventure! One thing I have not been because of you is bored! Being married to you may have been my greatest challenge, but collectively, it has also become our greatest accomplishment! I'm thankful that out of our chaotic rubble has come a story of hope and redemption we can share with the world!

My son Chris: Thank you for taking the time out of your busy schedule to offer your artistic talent and enduring patience to create this book cover. The creative gift that God has blessed you with is astounding, and I pray it will bring you to places you never thought you would land.

My daughter Noelle: You gave me the best piece of advice when I was pondering how to write my story and you said, "Mom, just start writing." It was that simple phrase that helped me start putting the "pen to the paper" and ultimately made this book a reality! You are an inspiration!

Mom and dad: You had every right to choose the route of anger and resentment against Kevin. Instead you chose forgiveness and acceptance into the Sievert clan which set a godly precedent for the family. For that I am forever grateful.

Jim and Judi: Your graciousness when you took the kids and me into your home in Kirkland came at a time when we would otherwise have been completely destitute. Thank you for not asking anything in return.

I am so grateful you were there when we needed you most!

Roger and Kimberly: You deserve honor, for all those times my kids and I were welcome at your home on our weekend trips to "Camp Sheridan." Your home was more than a place for us to stay; it was a refuge of love and acceptance at a time when it was so needed. You are still those same people today, with the greatest gift of hospitality I have ever witnessed!

Bruce and Carol: When others left us shuddering out in the cold you welcomed us in with wide open arms and warm merciful hearts. You not only sent Kevin out with a blessing (amazing!) but you sent me out with a pocket full of cash to start my new life in Oregon. This is the fullness of God's love in action! Your kind deeds will never be forgotten!! You are Jesus' hands on this earth!

My friend Sherri Purdy: You are one of my sheroes! Thank you for being there like no other friend when we first landed in Corvallis and no one knew how to handle us! You have prayed with me and stayed with me all the way! We have cried together and laughed together. Hopefully, we will continue to do a whole lot more laughing together. I love you dearly!

Gwen and Jerry: Your friendship has been invaluable in so many ways! You've not only counseled us in our turbulent times but you've offered support in our lives and business. The belief you have in us truly helps us believe in ourselves. What a privilege to do life with you guys!

Table of Contents

A NOTE FROM THE AUTHOR III

DEDICATION IV

ACKNOWLEDGEMENTS V

THE BACK STORY 1

UNUSUAL BEGINNINGS.. 1

LIFE IN THE DESERT 4

THE MOVE 5

A HOME ON HOLLYWOOD HILL 6

HOPES DASHED 8

THE DECISION THAT CHANGED OUR LIVES 11

A DISTRACTION 11

THE CONSULTING PROJECT 13

BACK ON TOP... 16

THE KNITTED BLANKET.. 17

CEASE AND DESIST 18

STRIPPED OF EVERYTHING 20

HOUSE RAID 20

THE PLEA BARGAIN 23

BLINDSIDED 25

VOLUNTARY SURRENDER 27

LETTERS FROM A PRISONER..31

SUDDENLY SINGLE... 31

THE DARKEST HOUR... 39

THE SAMURAI SWORD 43

COMMUNICATION AT LAST 48

THE FIRST VISIT 51

THROWING THE FIRST STONE 53

DEATH IN THE CEMETERY 64

FIRED! 68

BITTER TO BETTER **73**

A PLACE OF PEACE 73

HEAVENLY GIFTS 79

LITTLE LAMBS 82

LILIES OF THE FIELD 90

THE MAN IN THE VINEYARD 95

GOD'S OCEAN OF GRACE 99

THE FINISH LINE 104

RELEASE DATE 108

THE ROAD TO REDEMPTION **117**

HARD LANDING 117

A STRONG FOUNDATION 120

TWO SIMPLE VERBS 124

MORE THAN CONQUERORS 127

OUR PURPOSE UNVEILED 130

ROAD BLOCKS 132

GRIT AND VULNERABILITY 136

REFLECTIONS 140

CONCLUSION **143**

WORKS CITED **147**

The Back Story

If somebody had told me that one day my beloved husband of fifteen years would become an unwitting accomplice in the state of Washington's largest stock fraud, I would have laughed in a mixture of scoffing and disbelief. But it happened...*to me*. Here is my story.

UNUSUAL BEGINNINGS

From the moment Kevin reached out his hand to shake my own in welcome, I had an uncanny sense that this guy would be my husband. We met in a small campus ministry service in Davis, California, in the late 1980's. It was my first time in attendance. The minister paused the service for a short meet-and-greet and Kevin and I, standing directly across from each other, simultaneously reached out our hands. During the brief handshake and exchange of our names, I heard an inner voice say, "This man is going to be your husband."

I walked back to my seat puzzled as to why I would even have such a thought, since just a few months earlier, after graduating from college in Oregon, I had made an inner vow to be single and free. After my solemn pledge, I packed everything I cared about in my small hatchback and headed to Davis, California, to work with the pastors of a growing campus ministry. I believed a man would only distract me in my relatively new "born again" experience with Jesus and I wanted to focus solely on helping other girls come to the new freedom I had found.

After this brief encounter with Kevin, I couldn't help but wonder why I would have such a strong intuition about someone I didn't even know. Yet over the next couple weeks, being part of a small church community caused our paths to cross in ways that were unavoidable. I began to get some of my questions answered about him. You know, those mental boxes each of us have that we want to check off in order for it to be ok to like someone?

Was he handsome? Check. In a unique way he was handsome with his reddish-brown hair and blue eyes. Was he musical like I was? Check. He played the trumpet and was learning guitar.

Was he adventurous and fun? Seemed so. From what I knew this far, I could check those boxes, too.

But the thing that attracted me the most was his entrepreneurial spirit. The first time Kevin and I really broke through the surface was the night I locked my keys in my car.

It was a foggy, misty night in Sacramento, California. I was attending a Christian conference event with two of my friends, Kevin and Donna. At the close of the service, I suddenly realized I had locked my keys in my car. I reluctantly asked Kevin for help getting into my '76 orange Datsun B210. Boy was he glad I asked! Doesn't every guy want to rescue the girl?

Within minutes of using a bent-up wire through a small crack in the lining of the window, Kevin popped the lock and I was good to go. Only, I didn't go. We stood outside of my car in that dimly lit parking lot for at least an hour. To this day, I have the picture etched in my brain of the two of us talking, laughing, and tasting the "fresh, squeezed orange juice" that he was peddling out of the back of his car. (Yep, that's an entrepreneur for ya!) Finally, we said our good-byes and we each drove off having our own reaction to what had just happened.

But I was priding myself in my fierce independence (though I couldn't even break into my own car) and so I vowed to wipe all of this off my mind and move on with my "amazing" single life. Yet no matter how hard I tried NOT to think about this guy, I couldn't help but be attracted to his work ethic, love for God, and willingness to do whatever it took to start a business venture.

Needless to say, the idea of the two of us together was growing on Kevin too! Over the course of the next several months, many strange "coincidences" happened that would bring us even closer. Our campus group had a Christmas gift exchange and Kevin mysteriously drew my name. Sometimes we would get together with a pack of friends for cards or games and after everyone paired up for doubles; guess who was left? I could strongly attest to the hand of Providence orchestrating our lives in the big scheme of things, and it wasn't long before we were engaged.

Kevin still tells the story about how he asked me to marry him on our first official date. (I would not recommend this strategy, however, as it does have its shortfalls.) After all, why wait if we both felt deeply about each other and the sense that Divine Destiny had brought us together? Ironically, we were married exactly one year from the day that we first shook each other's hands.

LIFE IN THE DESERT

After marriage and a brief stint in California, Kevin and I moved to Mesa, Arizona, to be closer to Kevin's family and a business opportunity that led him into co-owning one of the largest Century 21 real estate offices in fast-growing Maricopa County. While he was cutting his entrepreneurial teeth on the real estate industry, I spent a couple of years working several receptionist jobs in order to bring home a paycheck. Soon a door opened for me to get a job in a small private school teaching preschoolers, which was my true passion.

Over the next several years, we were blessed with two healthy children, Christopher and Noelle. Oh, the wonderful advantages of having grandparents and cousins close by! We have many fond memories of holiday and birthday parties at Grandma and Papa's house with the young cousins, playing hide and seek in the air-conditioned house, and learning how to swim at an early age in the backyard pool.

But the constantly warm and sunny weather, and the dry, cactus-ridden landscape, grew mundane. After ten years of this arid climate, I longed for the lush green forests of the beautiful Northwest where I grew up. I looked forward to each summer, as our family would travel to the Seattle-Tacoma area to visit my parents during the picture-perfect days of July and early August. This region of the Northwest is the antithesis of the Phoenix area in both geography and climate with its massive Puget Sound island-dappled body of water, lakes scattered throughout the region, and heavily forested hills which are kept moist as it rains more than half the days of the year. Each time we took that trip, it was a little harder to return home to the brown, dusty, desert, with temperatures well over a hundred, and a blaring air conditioner.

I had been praying for quite some time that a business opportunity would arise in order for us to make a big move back to what I refer to as the "family hub". Kevin was fairly established with his plethora of business contacts and a steady income stream as the owner of a seminar business called Real Estate Technology Institute (RETI). I had no doubt that he had the moxie to operate a business anywhere we went, so our location need not be an issue. Furthermore, it would not be difficult for me obtain another teaching position in a preschool or kindergarten class. I was at peace, believing that our future was in God's hands and in His timing an opportunity would arise.

THE MOVE

In the spring, Kevin informed me he was selling his company, RETI, to a publicly traded real estate service provider called Homeseekers.com who would now employ him. The management of this new company preferred that we would relocate to either the headquarters in Brea, California, or the sales offices in Reno, Nevada. Kevin negotiated with them to allow him to work from home and commute to the different offices when needed. They also granted our request to relocate to the Seattle area. With all the traveling Kevin was doing throughout the United States, it didn't really make a difference where we lived as long as he was in proximity of a major airport; he could set up a home office virtually anywhere. Our break had finally come!

The next three weeks were truly a whirlwind of selling our home, having garage sales, saying goodbyes, and packing up the last twelve years of our lives in our minivan and a moving truck. I remember having a meltdown as I packed, not because I would miss living in Arizona, but because I was completely exhausted! Unfortunately, we still had a two-day journey ahead of us before we would reach our final destination and get some much-needed rest.

A HOME ON HOLLYWOOD HILL

Using my parent's house for base camp, we began to explore the Puget Sound area with the intention of finding an ideal place to settle. It didn't take long to fall in love with a hilly, charming town east of Seattle called Woodinville. Woodinville was a growing bedroom community with stately wineries, concerts on the lawns, home-pressed apple cider for sale, and gigantic million-dollar homes at the top of a great hillside overlooking the valley below. So with our kids and a map, we drove all over those hills with our print-out of rentals to guide us.

When we got to the crest of the hill, although not the street with the gigantic homes, we came to our next rental option: a light yellow ranch house sitting atop an acre lot with a long, upward-sloped driveway that eventually leveled out at a circle in front of the garage. There were large firs scattered throughout the grassy yard, yet it was cleared enough around the home to let the sunlight in. Behind and to the left of the home was a recently finished detached office with stepping stones from the house. When he wasn't traveling, Kevin would be able to step out the back door each morning and be at his office in about ten seconds!

Soon after taking up residence on what we came to know as Hollywood Hill, we enrolled the kids in a local private Christian school where I got a job as an assistant teaching in the preschool class. Kevin continued working for Homeseekers, traveling around the United States giving presentations to help real estate professionals market themselves on the fast-growing World Wide Web! (Now that's a blast from the past!)

That first year flew by. Before the conclusion of our rental term, Kevin was able to borrow enough of his restricted Homeseekers stock portfolio for a substantial deposit on a new home. We soon found a beautiful home for sale in an upscale neighborhood, not far from our rental, and wrote up a contract. After ten years in the desert and then a year in a rental, we could put down some roots in a wonderful community. I was thrilled!

HOPES DASHED

But things took a downward turn. This was the "Dot com" era (later referred to as Dot bomb!), and many had forecasted the financial bubble would eventually burst. And for us, that is exactly what happened. Kevin had received a strange call from the vice-chairman of Homeseekers. He pleaded with Kevin not to sell his stock. He said that if the market sees the upper management selling off stock portfolios, the business would sink. Apparently, one of the investors who had promised ten million dollars to the company had pulled out. And there was no one else willing to take the risk of funding the business. Being the loyal co-worker that he was, Kevin agreed to hang on to his shares. It turned out that the vice-chairman's buddy, also a significant shareholder, knew a crash was coming and immediately sold his entire portfolio! The company could not withstand the hit. Soon after, the company closed its doors, and everyone else lost their stock as well as their jobs.

Our year-long lease was coming to an end and the people who owned the house needed us out; their contract had ended with their out-of-state jobs and they were ready to move back home. After losing our stock, the contract on the new home purchase had to be rescinded and dealing with the sellers was not pleasant. Basically we felt as if we had just gotten spanked and had to run away with our tail between our legs. It was shameful and humiliating.

Kevin found us a condo to rent in a new development about ten minutes northwest of the hill called Pinnacle Sonata. He wanted me to be on board with it, so we first drove down to the complex without the kids. I still remember the sign had musical notes on it as if it were something to sing about. I was so sad I could hardly even look at the place. My dream of the forever home for us had slipped away like a leaf down a river and what I was facing now was nothing short of depressing.

The condos were stacked like matchboxes in row after row of sameness. It was obvious by the tiny shrubs and small trees, being held up by stakes and ropes planted in a haphazard fashion throughout the grounds, that they hadn't been open for occupancy very long. I became even less interested after the rep showed us a couple of units. Kevin kept trying to convince me that this would only be temporary but I was still licking my wounds. And instead of consoling me, this place made me feel even more removed from my hope of finding a place that we could call our own.

I felt I had no choice but to accept my circumstances and try to make the best of them. *Things can always be worse; this place is only temporary*, I reasoned. Well, it didn't take long after living there to find out that Pinnacle Sonata, although new, was not well-built. Some of the units' stair posts were actually cracking and breaking in pieces! There were complaints of structural issues all around the complex from shoddy construction. Then one day, one of my kids flushed the toilet upstairs in our unit and the ceiling started to leak on the kitchen table down below!

Furthermore, the walls seemed to have very poor insulation. And unfortunately, we shared a wall with a violent and abusive neighbor. Sometimes, when we all went to bed, Kevin and I could hear the degrading language spewing from this man's mouth while he cursed out the woman and her son who lived with him. On these horrific nights, I would lie in bed and pray our dear little children were asleep and wouldn't hear his hateful, violent rants. One day a police car drove up, there was a bit of a scuffle, and then I watched as they put handcuffs on the man and led him away in the patrol car. I tried to console the pre-teenage boy but felt my words were like a small band-aid on a badly bruised and wounded heart.

In spite of the trials, and detesting this place, I drew from my faith to believe this experience would be merely a stepping stone to something better. We would get out of this rut! I chose not to harbor resentment or anger towards my husband. After all, it seemed his fault that we were all here. But we were still a family and we were together! And I was determined to dig my heels in and make it through this setback.

The Decision That Changed Our Lives

A DISTRACTION

The financial climate back in 2000-2001 started booming. Microsoft, Nintendo, and AT&T were all located in nearby Redmond, Washington, and employed thousands of people, providing them with hearty incomes. Furthermore, in the late 80's, Microsoft had been offering stock options to their full-time employees. We heard through the real estate industry that the Seattle area had one of the highest rates of millionaires per capita. Many young Microsoft businessmen who had sold their shares and become millionaires were now buying pricey real estate and retiring young.

Kevin had run into someone who was interested in partnering with him in a Windermere Real Estate office. Selling came naturally to Kevin, and having previously owned the thirteenth largest Century 21 Real Estate franchise in Mesa, Arizona, this seemed the most logical direction to go. He would begin working on his Washington broker's license while developing his real estate business and clientele. Fortunately, we had enough savings to hold us over while he was in transition. I was relieved that things were looking up, and I could again hope to have a home soon for our family in our beautiful Northwest surroundings.

One early evening, Kevin came home from work and said he had met with a friend from church named Wes. Kevin and Wes had been drawn to each other because of their entrepreneurial interests and they frequently met for coffee to discuss business endeavors. Kevin went on to tell me that Wes had informed him of a company called Health Maintenance Centers (HMC), of which Wes was a shareholder. He also explained to Kevin that his good friend, Conrad, was the treasurer. According to Wes, HMC was currently offering stock at a dollar a share through what was known as the "friends and family round" (a company's first round of funding), and was projected to open on a large scale when it went public on Wall Street. Wes was going to pull some strings with his treasurer buddy to enable Kevin to purchase some stock. Kevin continued to rave about his conversation.

But I had a hard time listening. "So I thought you were going to use your money to get your real estate business up and running? I feel like this is just going to be a distraction," I answered. My response was not what he wanted to hear. All I did was annoy him. And I was frustrated that he had started heading in what seemed like the right direction with the real estate industry, and now that was about to be thwarted! We had just fallen flat on our bellies after losing our stock with Homeseekers and I didn't want to go there again.

The rest of the evening was tense. And in spite of the way I felt, Kevin invested ten grand into the company.

THE CONSULTING PROJECT

Not long after Kevin's original discussion about the mysterious new company, and the friends and family round stock options, he came home and shared some more news with me. Wes had called Kevin and told him Kevin Lawrence, the CEO of the company (who we referred to as Lawrence), wanted to speak with Kevin about a consulting project. Wes wondered if he could give Kevin's number to Lawrence. Kevin agreed. Again, I was indifferent.

The next day as he was driving home from Seattle, Lawrence called. After pulling his car over to the side of the road, they talked for nearly an hour. Lawrence explained the history of HMC, (later called Znetix), all of the big shots and celebrities involved, and where they were headed with the initial public offering. He told Kevin he needed help setting up and organizing a formal investor relations department.   Furthermore, Kevin said, Lawrence needed someone to develop a process for handling investor inquiries, and to verify all of the investor records—of which there were thousands. Lawrence had told him the current investor database was a mess and needed cleaning up.

"Lawrence is offering me a $15,000 consulting fee for thirty days!" Kevin boasted. "After that he said he'll put me on call for half that rate for another 90 days. And by then the company will have gone public." But

I was full of suspicion and doubt. I knew in my gut that when something sounds too good to be true it probably isn't true. "I don't think you should do this!" I told him. "Why not?" he challenged. "Because I don't have a good feeling about this," I replied. "And besides that, this isn't even your thing. You're good at real estate and I think you should continue to pursue that!"

Kevin's current opportunity with Windermere was going well, and I was perturbed that he would divert his course. I had also believed that it is never a good idea to make a decision solely based on money. When that's the case, money becomes your dictator!

But Kevin wasn't willing to listen, or better yet, to hear me; his mind was already made up. The train was already starting to roll down the tracks and I don't think anyone could have stopped it. And unfortunately, I was on that train by virtue of our marriage. The decision he had made would either affect our family positively or negatively. I sincerely doubted that anything positive would come out of this. Personally, I worried the train was headed for a crash.

Every time we were with friends, Kevin would speak zealously about HMC. He even persuaded several friends and family members to invest in shares, echoing the rumored statement, *"When it goes public, it's going to be a billion-dollar company."* I was sick. And I couldn't explain all the reasons why. It was an intuition.

Those first thirty days went by, then ninety, and then ninety more, during which time Kevin set up and managed the investor relations division for HMC from a swanky high-rise office building in prestigious Bellevue. There turned out to be such a plethora of investor records and inquiries that he had to hire six people to handle it all. The exorbitant monthly "consulting fee," plus bonuses and commissions for stock sales continued to roll in—much longer than Lawrence had originally suggested.

This is about the time I transitioned from being angry and cynical to being glad I was a beneficiary of this endeavor, be it right or be it wrong. I realize now, this was where I began to err in my thinking. My rationale was, *"I may not have agreed with Kevin's job decision but I could soothe my wounds when I allowed myself to partake in the benefits of making this much money."* We had signed a one-year lease with Pinnacle Sonata and the end of the term was approaching. By now we had enough income to support a mortgage payment, but with the competitive housing market in the Seattle area, we needed a significant down payment for the kind of home we desired. We began our search.

One of my acquaintances at our church was a realtor named Sarah. We met with Sarah, told her what we were looking for, and gave her our budget. Soon after our meeting with Sarah, Kevin spoke to Lawrence and let him know we were in the market for a new home. Lawrence agreed to help with the down payment. *"What?"* I thought, *"Who does that? I mean, what kind of business owner pays the down payment on a house for an employee?"* This should've been a huge red flag for both Kevin and me. But unfortunately, we were eager to accept his "gracious" offer.

BACK ON TOP

Sarah took us up to the crest of a hill in Bothell, Washington (*yes, once again a hill*) to a listing that was in a subdivision called The Promontory. The Promontory was a neighborhood of about 35 homes ranging from $500,000-$800,000. We drove to the home in a cul-de-sac, and although it had a small front yard, Sarah assured us that there was a sloping green space behind the home on which no one else could build. We were interested.

Now if the home we wanted to purchase on Hollywood Hill was grand, this was even grander! It was a three-story home with a massive entry, a chef's dream kitchen, and two huge decks off the back of the house. Looking straight out from the main floor, you had a stunning view of the Cascade Mountains on the eastern horizon. The basement was like an apartment in-and-of- itself with a completely finished second kitchen next to a media area with—no kidding—a disco ball! We fell in love! And with Lawrence and his company paying the entire down payment as a generous "bonus," it was a no-brainer. The seller accepted our contract.

I began to breathe a sigh of relief after we relocated to our new home in The Promontory. Our kids made friends with the neighbor kids down the street who went to the same school. Noelle and her girlfriends played with Barbie Dolls for hours in the sprawling basement, and Chris and his new buddy played video games or explored the green belts surrounding the subdivision. We got our first dog which the kids affectionately named Carmel Frappuccino.

After summer break, I went back to work when school started, where I had been assisting in the preschool of a nearby elementary school where my children attended. We even had a church group meeting in our home one evening every week. We had pot lucks with the neighbors in the summer at the Promontory common space. Life seemed to take on a state of rhythm and normalcy, at least for the kids and me. If only I would've known it was the calm before the storm!

THE KNITTED BLANKET

Kevin would often come home with strange news about the company. One particular day in October 2001, one year into what was projected to be a thirty-day position with HMC, he told me the Investor Relations Department would not be getting their paychecks. *"What?"* I asked, *"What's going on?"* His answer was not satisfying. By this time I had noticed several red flags, but this one seemed the most obvious. I mean, what kind of legitimate company cannot pay their people?

I got that same sick feeling inside. We had taken a big risk on this home and with big risks come big falls. I didn't want to lose another home. Especially now, since we were living there! I remember falling across my king-sized bed and crying out to God! *"Help, Lord! What's going on? Please, show me!"*

I hadn't prayed long when I got a mental picture of a knitted blanket. I remembered all of us getting knitted blankets from Grandma for Christmas one year. I saw in my mind's eye someone pulling the main thread. As he or she pulled the thread, the blanket started unraveling and unraveling till there was nothing but a pile of thread on the floor. No more blanket. I got that sick feeling again. I knew without a doubt on that day that symbolically, HMC was that blanket. And it was coming apart at the seams! I told Kevin about the vision but even though he had his own doubts about the company, it wasn't enough to convince him to jump off the speeding train.

CEASE AND DESIST

Kevin attempted to research the state of HMC on his own, as well as seek out answers from legal personnel, but he was never given a definitive conclusion. Lawrence constantly eluded everyone. Kevin and his two work buddies, who had never seen Lawrence in person, decided to show up and "catch" Lawrence without warning in his office on Bainbridge Island. But when they arrived, only the secretary was there, who ironically said Lawrence was like the Wizard of Oz.

Where was he? Was he really just a con hiding behind a curtain? Was he running a fraudulent business? And if so, why were there thousands of investors and so many celebrities involved in the company? If this was not for real, then how could so many people be duped at the same time? There was always a shroud of mystery over everything. Kevin could not find indelible proof that there was criminal activity going on...until the Washington State Security and Exchange Commission got involved.

One day in April of 2001, the State of Washington's Department of Financial Institutions (DFI), Securities Division ordered a cease and desist against Lawrence and HMC, Inc. According to the DFI, Lawrence had violated securities codes. The decree was published in the local newspapers and the news traveled rapidly from coast to coast throughout the investor community.

Predictably, Lawrence had an explanation for everything. He informed Kevin and the investor relations department that he would simply pay the violation fines, restructure the business, and finish the project. But Kevin wasn't buying it. Both of our suspicions turned to fear.

Stripped of Everything

HOUSE RAID

Knock, knock, knock, knock, knock!

One morning at around 7:00 am, we awoke to an abrupt pounding on our door. It was a school morning and our kids were already up so Chris opened the door. *"Dad, there are a bunch of people here to see you,"* he yelled. Kevin quickly threw on some sweats and a t-shirt and went downstairs to the foyer. Four men and a woman, all wearing long grey and black trench coats, flashed their badges and bullied their way in. They handed Kevin a subpoena and explained they were searching for anything and everything involving Lawrence or his company. They searched Kevin's office, grabbing the computer, files, papers; they took anything they could get their hands on. They even opened the safe, and grabbed a bundle of cash— several thousand dollars. I was furious that they could just reach in and take our money! This would come back to haunt me later.

From that day forward, we discovered that all of our accounts were frozen. None of our credit cards worked. They put a lien on our house. We didn't have fancy cars or loads of money in some foreign bank account, but that's not what the government thought.

News articles began to come forth in the Seattle Times about the SEC and FBI involvement in HMC, Inc., and Znetix. It was reported that Lawrence had bilked upwards of $74 million dollars from investors. It was also reported that *"Kevin McCarthy, an accomplice, had stashed millions of dollars in overseas tax shelters!"* (The FBI later proved that rumor to be false.) The news and rumors spread, and our name and reputation were completely tarnished.

The investors were seething. Many of them had "sold the farm" and put everything they had into HMC/Znetix stock. Many of our new friends now despised us, and some of them turned their backs on us and scorned us. Lawrence's first name was also Kevin which made things worse. Many of the horrible things Kevin Lawrence had perpetrated were pinned to Kevin McCarthy because the journalists would mix up their names. The waters were muddied, and Kevin was dragged down with Lawrence, whether he actually committed the rumored crimes or not. It was a classic case of "guilty by association."

I was so emotionally distraught I couldn't think straight. When a friend called to console me, I couldn't even talk; all I could do was sob. I wanted to do anything I could not to be recognized in public. Thoughts rushed through my mind of dying my hair brown (I am a blond), cutting it short, and wearing thick, black glasses and a bulky coat. Better yet, I wanted the earth to open up and swallow me whole. It was the most humiliating thing I have ever, and am sure will ever experience.

Right about that time, I threw my back out by pulling weeds on my backyard slope and I had to see a chiropractor. When I arrived at the chiropractic office, the assistant told me to take everything off in the small changing room and put the hospital-like garment on that tied in the back. "*Seriously? At a chiropractor's office?*" I remember thinking, *"This is my life. I'm being stripped of everything."* Little did I know that this was just the beginning.

Kevin had originally sought a criminal attorney to assist and defend him in the pre-indictment process. Certainly if he had a competent attorney, he could prove his innocence, be exonerated, and move on with his life. But the attorney he intended to hire laid the reality on him that because of the enormity of the case, Kevin wouldn't be able to afford him (especially after the government froze all of our assets.) So inevitably, a court-appointed attorney named Carol would be his defender.

Kevin and Carol had many meetings with one another to gradually unravel Kevin's involvement in what was now being hailed as the state of Washington's largest stock fraud case in history. Kevin would come home after those interrogative meetings looking and sounding like he had been in a boxing ring with a heavyweight. In fact, I have never personally witnessed that much stress on anyone; I was worried he could have a heart attack at any moment! I now understand how heavy periods of stress can really take a toll on a person.

Kevin would share his disparaging meetings with me, about how he and Carol were in no way seeing eye-to-eye. He didn't know it at the time, but Carol was intentionally testing his resolve in order to know the truth of his involvement. He was completely exasperated.

THE PLEA BARGAIN

During one of the grueling meetings with his attorney, Kevin received some devastating news. Carol told Kevin that the best plea bargain the government was offering him was a *ten-year* prison term. The plea consisted of one conspiracy to commit securities fraud, mail fraud, wire fraud and a money-laundering charge which provided a maximum five-year sentence. Carol explained that in order to get to a ten-year plea offer, the government added another count of mail fraud, which also had a five-year maximum sentence.

Kevin was furious. Carol was trying to convince him that ten years was a *gift*. She relayed to him that if he were to go to trial and lose, he would be eligible for the same charges and sentence as his boss. Based on the Federal Minimum Sentencing Guidelines point system, Lawrence would be sentenced to 25-30 years. Kevin was holding on to his resolve that he was innocent. But Carol was emphatic, "*Kevin, are you gonna take the plea bargain or not?*" Kevin fired back, "*Carol, there's no way I'm going to admit I was guilty. I did not know my boss was committing a crime! I will not accept the plea bargain!*" Then an epiphany came.

"Hmm," Carol said, "I just realized why we are not seeing eye-to-eye. You're seeing this through a moral perspective and I'm seeing this through a legal perspective. I believe you now that you didn't know that your boss was committing a crime. I can even convince the jury of the same. Unfortunately, from a legal perspective, in the federal statutes, ONLY ONE PERSON IN A CONSPIRACY NEEDS TO KNOW A CRIME IS BEING COMMITTED. You see, Kevin, you'll never win in court if you try to plead your innocence! And you'll do a whole lot more prison time than ten years!"

That was the day we were shaken to our very core. We realized we were holding squirt guns and the prosecuting attorneys involved in the case had bazookas. The judge presiding over the case was reputably strict and by-the-book. And the climate for corporate crime was heated by the recent notorious Enron scandal and President Bush shouting, "Hard time for white collar crime!" on national media. As a result, the Feds were cracking down hard on corporate crime.

It was time for us to stop bucking the system and concede. According to the law, Kevin *was guilty*. There really was no way out. The choice before him was to accept a ten-year prison sentence or face the legal firing squad with a high risk of getting sentenced to even more time. I couldn't believe my own ears when I told Kevin he needed to fall at their mercy and take the plea bargain before they rescinded the offer.

Carol had relayed to Kevin that sometimes the judge will soften if he or she gets letters in favor of the defendant, attesting to his character and asking for leniency. So we began to ask friends and family to write. Since Kevin had no previous convictions, putting a letter together of this sort was not a difficult task. The letters flooded in. One of them even attested to the fact that Kevin was an usher at the church the writer attended. Ushers handle parishioner's offerings and there was never any doubt that Kevin had counted and then channeled the money where it should go. All of the letters were positive and the writers hoped they would help in persuading the judge.

Kevin also rallied our friends and family to attend the sentencing. Carol suggested that seeing lots of folks deeply concerned about his welfare and attesting to his character was another factor that may possibly convince the judge to shorten the sentence. In addition, Kevin was fully cooperating with the government as somebody on the inside who could help them develop the case. We anticipated that all these factors would play out in our favor. Family and friends that remained close to us joined us in prayer that the term of the plea bargain would be greatly reduced. We all clung to hope.

BLINDSIDED

Kevin's original sentencing date had been pushed back several times. Each time, the prosecutor said he needed more evidence on the case against Lawrence, so the sentencing would be rescheduled. Once again, the sentencing was scheduled for the upcoming Tuesday and Carol had told Kevin to prepare for another cancellation. No phone calls were made to our support group of family and friends. After all, this had happened at least three times prior. But Tuesday rolled around and there was no cancellation! It was too short of a notice to expect anyone else to come so Kevin and

I took the long, sobering drive to the Seattle courthouse—*alone.*

When we walked into the courtroom, it was surprisingly empty. On the left were Carol and her assistant sitting at one table, and on the right at the other table were the prosecuting attorney and his assistant. The judge sat just above eye level in the front with the typical full-length black gown and a smug look on her face. Beside her on the lower level were the bailiff and the court reporter. There was only one other man with a note pad on his lap sitting in the back, presumably a journalist from a Seattle newspaper, tracking the case. Carol motioned for Kevin to enter through the wooden gate, while I took a seat somewhere in the middle. Not even one of the many supporters we had rallied together was there. Why should they be? This was all supposed to be postponed! It felt like a setup. I had a terrible feeling that this wasn't going to go well.

The exchange of questions and answers that followed was brief and to the point. After the judge verified that Kevin did indeed sign the ten-year plea bargain, she asked the prosecutor for his sentencing recommendation. The prosecutor asked that Kevin serve forty-eight months. Carol then countered with forty months. The judge refused. Instead, she vocalized her disdain for white-collar crime by accepting the prosecutor's request of forty-eight months. She then said some very nasty words about Kevin's lack of "moral center," and her disregard for the letters she had received from our supporters. Lastly, she told Kevin he was to report to the Sheridan

Federal Correctional Institution in Oregon in thirty days—and then she slammed her gavel down!

Kevin and I looked at each other in horror. We couldn't believe what had just happened! It had to be a bad dream from which I would awake. *"Will somebody please tell me this is really not happening? Please! Please! This can't be happening!"* My mind screamed.

But it *did* happen. I can recall the long drive home, back across the 520 bridge to the east side. There weren't words. Only cries. Out of the depths of my soul came cries. Then questions. *How would we tell our kids? Our families? Friends? Four years! Four long, long years!* Our son Christopher was 13, and our daughter Noelle was only 11. How would they ever understand this? *These are the most critical years of their lives to be without their dad. And what about prison in Oregon? We live in Washington! I can't believe I am even using the P word!*

I have never stood on the edge of a cliff of uncertainty the way I did that day. That day, the contents of our lives were thrown upside down and EVERYTHING had to be sorted out.

VOLUNTARY SURRENDER

For the next thirty days, we tried as hard as we could to cling to every moment. And although Kevin and I were constantly aware of the impending doom, thankfully the kids were blissfully unaware as they enjoyed their summer fun. The court had ordered Kevin to *voluntarily surrender* to the Federal prison in Sheridan, Oregon, on August 9, 2004 at 12:00 pm.

There were no handcuffs, no police escort, no bail, and not even a phone call from the authorities; there was just a date and time on the calendar for Kevin to check in at the designated address. It felt as if it were something we signed up for, like summer camp, instead of something we were ordered by the court of law to do. Certainly there must be convicted felons who take advantage of the freedom to voluntarily surrender and decide not to cooperate. But after almost two years of waiting till all the court dust settled, we shared a strange feeling of relief that the day was finally approaching. We could go from *awaiting time*, to *doing time*.

Voluntary surrender day arrived. The drive to Sheridan was about a five-hour drive south from the East side of Seattle, through Portland, Oregon, and then southwest to the prison. While in the car, we discussed Kevin's concerns for me: being a single mom, supporting the family, getting a full-time job, taking care of all of the bills, and enduring the added stress of driving five hours on the weekend to visit him. There was less discussion about him and his home-to-be for the next four years. His environment would be much more predictable: three square meals a day, an issue of clothing and shoes, no real big decisions to make, no kids to parent, no cars to maintain, no health insurance to pay, and in fact, no bills to pay at all! All basic needs would be met by the Bureau of Prisons (BOP).

In contrast, I would be living with my in-laws in a rental home in Kirkland, Washington, until I could find a higher-paying job and afford to get out on our own. The home was small with three bedrooms on the main floor for my mother and father-in-law, Chris and Noelle, and a tiny room upstairs that I would occupy. I would have to transfer Chris and Noelle from the school they loved to the local public schools. I had been left with an insurmountable pile of debt and bills. The FBI had taken our extra cash. My credit was destroyed, thanks to the seizure of our home and all of our assets. Furthermore, the kids did not in any way understand what was happening or deserve what was happening. They were the innocent victims who had to face the scrutiny from friends and school kids. At this time and place, life did not seem fair. Kevin wasn't the only one paying for the "conspiracy to commit fraud." The kids and I were as well.

Finally, we passed the *"Federal Correctional Institution Ahead- 1 Mile"* sign and I felt that familiar sickness in the pit of my stomach. After taking the exit, we passed another sign that read *"Sheridan Cemetery."* I thought to myself, *"How appropriate, a prison with a cemetery right beside it, so when they die in prison they have a place to bury them."* After passing the cemetery, we took a left turn into the prison compound. The road we turned onto was flanked by two completely different-looking complexes. The one on the right was a large maximum-security federal prison for male inmates. This prison was encased by a twenty-foot fence with another ten feet of razor wire at the top. A tower stood to the left of the building with a guard who had visible access to all sides. In front of the secure area of the prison was a building for entry with a small parking lot.

On the left side was more of a college campus-looking complex with a set of several buildings. They looked like dorms painted white with orange roofs instead of the usual grey block walls. I saw no fences around these buildings, only cement walkways and a parking area. This was the minimum-security Federal Prison Camp (yes, that is really the name,) also for male offenders. To the west of these buildings were fields with crops in them. (We would find out later that the prison started an agriculture program to provide produce to the prison and other nearby prisons while taking advantage of cheap labor.)

We slowly made our way to the prisoner in-processing building on the right (gulp). The whole place smacked of fear and intimidation. Though I wanted to say a meaningful good-bye, everything inside of me wanted to run away from there. I was more than ready to slam the gas pedal to the floor, drive out that main road, past that Sheridan Cemetery with all its tombstones, and not look back. Our good-bye was short and awkward. And I was out of there.

Letters From a Prisoner

SUDDENLY SINGLE

Two days later, back in Kirkland, Washington, I received my first letter from Kevin.

It read:

Day 1   8/9/4

Dear Rachel, Chris and Noelle,

It's about 6:30 pm on my first night in my new house. It's been an interesting day. I'm part sad and a little intimidated. Sad because I already miss you all very much. I'm full of tears as I write wanting to kiss you all goodnight and say, "I love you, see you in the morning, goodnight." But God is sustaining me as I'm sure He will you. I've already seen His mercy and grace today as you'll see when you read the diary of my day. I hope and pray I'll be home in six months. (Kevin and I were hoping against all odds that he would still be vindicated through an appeal and his sentence would be overturned and he would be home in six months.) But if not, there is a lot of work to be done here as well. I'm fully

31

surrendered to God's will and purpose in all this- as you should be as well. I look forward to seeing you all next weekend.

So here's how my day went today. Mom dropped me off at noon at what's called the Federal Detention Center. It's like a county jail where they in-process new prisoners. They brought me to a processing area and took more fingerprints and a photo. I was placed in a "holding cell" and after about 90 minutes, I saw the counselor and did some paperwork. About one more hour in the cell, and then I was seeing the doctor for routine questions about health. At 3:00 pm they walked me over to the Federal Prison Camp and showed me my new bed which is permanent until I leave. So, hallelujah, I never spent the night in the (medium security) jail.

The grounds are very nice. Even flower pots and landscaping. My new bed is in what is called "The Quad". There are eight quads per wing and eight wings per building. There are two buildings. I haven't met any in my wing that I would have wanted to meet in the streets. At 4:00 pm they had a "stand up" count. I have to stand by my bunk holding the ID card they made me and answer to roll call. No big deal. About 5:00 they called our unit for dinner.

After dinner I went back to the dorm and one of the guys told me I could get a free care package from the chapel. Great tip. I would and will recommend everyone entering prison to go right to the chapel. Here, I met some nice guys who were both in the last 5 years of 20 year sentences! They gave me a care package with toothbrush, toothpaste, shaving cream, razor, etc.

The one guy-Adam-walked me around and showed me some forms. I've enclosed the forms for you for visitation. After my tour I went back to the chapel from where I am now writing this letter. In the main chapel some prisoners are watching a movie on big screen.

More about the chapel: They have a protestant service on Sundays at 12:30 pm and a bible study prior to that. On Thursdays a volunteer from outside is leading in the chapel a bible study using the book "Purpose Driven Life." On Fridays some full Gospel businessmen fellowship volunteers lead a service. The guys I met and others pray in the chapel at 5:30 am each morning. I will be spending a lot of time in the chapel reading and studying.

I can make a maximum of 300 minutes of personal calls per month at my expense. It will take several days to get a card and pin #. I don't know the cost of the card. I'm required to fill out a list in advance of all phone numbers I wish to call (up to 30 numbers on the list). I cannot discuss business matters at all! Calls are limited to 15 minutes and we have to wait 60 minutes between calls.

*Visiting hours are generous: Mondays and Fridays 6-8:00 pm and Saturday and Sundays from 8:30am-

3:00pm. Everyone who wants to visit must be on the pre-approved visitor list.

*I'm looking forward to the weight rooms. They also have TV rooms, pool and ping pong, sports, hobbies and crafts like woodworking, etc.

*As for work, I was told to find a job ASAP. If I don't find a job, I will be stuck in the kitchen. Chapel jobs are hard to get but I'm believing for favor. No job is very hard though from what I'm told.

*Lights are out at 10 pm, but reading lights are allowed in your bunk anytime.

*The bathrooms are very modest-doors on stalls, private showers, etc. Quite surprising!

Well, that's all I can think of. Sorry to bore you with details. I know inquiring minds will want to know.

I love you guys with all my heart. Today was a victory. I am living above the circumstances, redefining normal. I did sing "It is well with my soul" when I first was in the holding room today. To God be the glory. I know in the heartache tonight longing for you all, God will show Himself strong as He will do for you as well.

I love you! Hugs and kisses!

Kevin (that's dad to you two!) (Grin)

Lots of emotions flooded my soul as I read the letter. Everything seemed so perfect. Three square meals, a chapel with a big screen, flower pots, sports and a weight room, for heaven's sake! I was starting to feel angry with his camp-like experience. *"I told him not to take the job. I had a bad feeling about it, but he did it anyway!"* I thought to myself. And the more I thought about his friendly surroundings, the madder I got. "He's not the one in prison, I am! I'm an adult with two kids living with my in-laws in a rental house! And he left me with his unpaid bills and a mountain of his debt! Yet I'm the one that has to clean up the mess and support the family." Somehow it didn't feel like true justice was meted out!

Two days later another letter came:

8/10/4

Hi Rachel,

It's about 6:00 pm and I'm in the chapel with headphones on listening to a Michael W. Smith video soundtrack writing you this letter.

Last night was a rough one as far as sleep. The dorm sounds like an earthquake with all the snoring. I have to figure out how to get some earplugs. I was also lonely for you and the kids. I miss you all so much, I couldn't bear to not talk to you or see you. Everyone says that visitors are key to getting by during your stay…something to look forward to each month or so. I hope you guys have a great time at the lake this weekend. It will be fun! I wish I were there. Tell Chris and Noelle I love them with all my heart. Dad will be home soon never to leave again until my final trip home to Jesus whenever that comes. Be excited for what God is doing. He has a plan. We're all part of it. Pray for me to stay strong, get into a routine and not be distracted by activities. Also pray I get an awesome job that allows me time to study. I love you!!!! Rach- You're the love of my heart and I long for our reunion.

Love, Kevin (Dad)

I knew I couldn't stay mad. Both Kevin and I had received a great deal of Bible study and teaching. I had given my life fully to Christ in college and made the decision I would "pick up my cross" and follow Him, no matter what that meant. I had trusted Him for the right husband and there was no doubt in my mind He had brought Kevin and me together. Even when the two of us had fought against the relationship for different reasons, circumstances just kept bringing us together. We had even sought counsel for our engagement in order to make sure we weren't making the wrong decision. In our marriage vernacular, divorce was not an option. We were committed to the "till death do us part, in sickness and in health" thing.

I knew the scriptures about forgiveness and "not letting the sun go down on your anger". I realized that harboring anger and unforgiveness toward Kevin would only cause me to become a bitter woman. *I had to forgive him*....even if it meant over and over again. For not listening to me...for caring more about the job and the promised shares of stock than what I thought! For having blinders on when the neon lights were flashing! For ignoring me and the kids! For making all that money and having nothing to show for it! NOTHING!!! Everything had been taken from us! The more I thought about it, the angrier I became. I was truly conflicted. It would be much easier to just "let him rot in jail." Let him learn his lesson on his own! For now, I tucked my feelings deep down inside and had to face the world.

I found out the hard way that one of our bank accounts was completely overdrawn. I hadn't realized Kevin had not taken care of the personal accounts before he left and made the proper transfers. And now, with no money coming in, the bills on auto-pay were bouncing. *"Just another one of his messes to clean up,"* I thought. *"Thanks a million!"*

We were also having computer issues. Kevin was the techie one of the home and as fate would have it, when he left, the computer went berserk. I made sure to write about it in a letter I wrote to him. Writing was an opportunity for me to get all the frustrations out. And he couldn't answer back. It felt pretty good!

On August 18th I received his response:

Hi Hun!

Sorry about the troubles at home with computers and banks. I never put money in the B of A account. I didn't think to check it before we left. I feel terrible that I had to leave you with the loose ends- there are probably

37

others? I know it's harder for you and the kids than for me. I pray for you always. I just love you so much for being a winner and for loving me through my faults and weaknesses. Read the book called the Heavenly Man. It is incredible. You'll appreciate our marriage even more.

I miss you terribly. I was very lonely today (Monday) after one week of zero communication with you. Then about 8 pm tonight they paged me to the office and handed me four pieces of mail—Yahoo!!! Happy Day!!! I cried as I read each one. Tears of joy in hearing from you all and tears of sadness for being apart. Hope we can see each other during visitor hours soon. I love you. I will be excited to see you, hug you, squeeze you, and kiss you.

Love, Kev

His first word was *sorry*. And he acknowledged my feelings. *Yes, it is harder for me and the kids—you got that right.* Furthermore, he acknowledged his "faults and weaknesses!" But even so, he had forgotten to transfer money to my account?! How do you just forget that? I was ticked. Financial loose ends from Kevin's absence were happening daily. Credit card companies who had gotten no answer from his defunct phone number were now calling my cell phone. This only made the pain worse, and my feelings of anger and resentment grew stronger.

Kevin had left me a folder of all of the bank account information, credit card debt, and unpaid bills.

We had so many bills and debtors that he had printed out a large ledger sheet listing every one of them and how much we owed each one. Looking over the sheet caused more stress than anything else I had to deal with so far. I had no idea we had incurred this much debt! One day, when no one was home and the creditors were calling, I put my head down over the folder on my in-law's kitchen table and cried out to God while sobbing uncontrollably, "*Lord!*" I cried, "*Please take my life! All I need is for you to send a semi-truck into my lane head-on and it'll be quick. Please, Lord!*" The debt folder became wet with my tears as I buried my head in my arms.

THE DARKEST HOUR

The darkness and despair I was feeling became even darker.

Inmates were allowed to make calls daily as long as they had phone privileges approved and money in their account. Kevin's phone use had not yet been approved so we still had no communication other than our letters. The visiting approval process took time. I had filled out the forms he sent me and mailed them back to Sheridan. The BOP would receive the paperwork and conduct a thorough screening and background check to make sure I wasn't on the convicted felon list. Then Kevin would be notified that I was approved and he would pass the info on to me via the letters. It was hard to imagine a life without cell phone communication and we were living it. There really was nothing efficient or predictable about the process of being approved; the administration had no reason to rush anything on behalf of the prisoners. We were completely at their mercy.

In one of the letters I received from Kevin, he relayed the information to me that the immediate family could come to visitation the first month *without* the background check. After receiving this new information I decided the kids and I would go and visit Kevin on his second weekend of *doing time*. I called a friend from college, Kimberly, who lived in Tualatin, Oregon, to see if we could spend a night at her place on Friday and then get up early on Saturday and drive to Sheridan, about an hour from her home. She cheerfully obliged and I made plans to take the four-hour drive from my temporary home in Kirkland, Washington, to her home in Tualatin after work on Friday.

The weekend came fast. And although I was still conflicted inside about so many things, I knew it would be positive for me to see Kevin and for the kids to see their dad. After all, this was the longest any of us had gone without any contact, other than the letters.

The drive was long and I was tired. But the kids and I cheered ourselves up on the road with fast food and loud music. We all embraced anything to lighten the mood.

My good friend, Kimberly, and her husband Roger, were the kind of people that fully lived out their faith by the love they showed towards whomever God brought their way. Not only did they receive us with open arms, but they served us with their warm hospitality and food. We were in good hands. Coming here was like salve on the wounds. There was no judgment, only kindness.

The morning came much too soon after chatting with Kimberly into the wee hours. All of the prisons have strictly-enforced rules about visitation and Kevin had written a warning about being there before 9:30 am. The BOP shuts down the visiting hours during the inmate count and they don't open them again until after 10:30 am. He also wrote that there can be lengthy lines to get into the visitor room and if the kids and I didn't get in position, we could be shut out. I was nervous as I got in the car at 7:30 am. There were so many unpredictable outcomes at this point and I wanted to make sure we made it in.

The *Federal Correction Institution* sign came up fast and before I knew it I was approaching the exit off of Highway 18 which, if you stayed on, eventually led to the beautiful Oregon Coast. I had visited many of the charming seaside towns lining the ocean in my late teens and early twenties with my family. Who would've thought in a thousand years this time I would be veering *off* the much more desired route to visit my *husband* in *prison? Oh my gosh! I could hardly believe I was doing this.* It seriously felt like I was living somebody else's life!

I drove up the two-way street past the shady cemetery and pulled into the complex behind a line of cars waiting to take a left into the already-filling parking area. I felt a nervous queasiness in my stomach as the questions flooded my mind. *What if we didn't get here soon enough? What if something's happened and Kevin can't come to the visitor center? What if the line is too long and we don't make it in? What if? What if?* Because of the fact that we

41

had had no communication, Kevin didn't know we were coming.

I parked and the kids and I headed toward the entryway. My heart was beating fast. Most of the people heading toward the building looked like veterans of the prison protocol, who all seemed to have the procedure down to a science. In contrast, I looked like the proverbial deer in the headlights. To make things more uncomfortable, the general mood of people gathering was awkwardly quiet and somber. I had the sensation again of wanting to turn around and run away. But like a good mom, I led my children into the building, filled out the required form, and got into the slow-moving line.

After what seemed like eternity, my kids and I came up to the counter. An unpleasant-looking man in a prison security uniform (referred to as "cops" by the inmates) asked for my paperwork and I handed him the completed form. I held my breath while he did his computer check for any criminal history I might have had. Quite some time passed and he looked up and said, "*I can't let you in.*" "*What? Why not?*" I asked, anxiously. He fired back, "*Because you're not pre-approved!*" My voice started to tremble, "*I was told that immediate family had one month to visit before they had to be approved.*" He started to get angry, "*I don't know who told you that, but they were wrong.*" "*But I just drove five hours to visit my husband and you're going to turn me and my kids away?*" My voice was quivering.

The cop had already moved on. There was no compassion, no apologies, nothing! Just the angry sound of his voice as he shouted, "*NEXT!*" My kids and I had no choice but to turn around and walk out.

"ASSHOLE!!!" I blurted out, as the door closed behind me. *"Mom!!"* My daughter said with a snicker. My kids had NEVER heard me swear before! But if ever there was an appropriate time to use an expletive to describe someone, this was it! I was livid that he would turn us away!

I drove off the complex with a plethora of emotions running through my veins. I looked down at my arms clutching the wheel and noticed I was shaking violently.   I was angry, hurt, disappointed, and so overwrought with emotion that I wanted to ram my car into a telephone pole. Fortunately, I had enough sense to pull over to the shoulder. Chris and Noelle were too afraid to say anything. We all just sat in the silence of our own thoughts for a while. I finally gained enough composure to steer back onto Highway 18 and head east to Kimberly's.

THE SAMURAI SWORD

By the time I pulled up in front of Kimberly's house my head was pounding! I had had little sleep, little to eat, and my stress level could not have been much higher. I was already a battered, weary soldier and the battle was just getting started. Kimberly welcomed the three of us in once again and offered us the same beds as the night before, a hot meal, and most of all, a place for consolation and rest.

After we ate, Kimberly asked if we wanted to see the movie *The Last Samurai.* Both sets of kids said yes, and I apathetically went along with the crowd as we all slumped down in her sectional. I was only half-listening when the scene came on with two young Samurai boys play-fighting in the rain with their wooden swords. After one of the boys drops his sword in defeat, the protagonist, Nathan (played by Tom Cruise,) picks up the sword and half-heartedly fights the little guy. Since he is obviously the larger and stronger person, Nathan simply catches the boy's sword with his hand. A Samurai tribal leader who has been watching them frolic walks up and asks Nathan to drop his sword. Nathan refuses, not just once, but twice. The dual is on! The expert Samurai warrior wields his sword with little effort defeating Nathan over and over and over and OVER! Finally, Nathan is left bloody and beaten, lying on his back in the pouring rain.

Suddenly it was as if everything in my life freeze-framed on this scene; my spiritual eyes were opened and I saw myself in a battle. I was that unskilled swordsman! I had a large sword in my hand, but because I didn't know how to use it, I had sustained several blows. I definitely felt wounded and powerless after what happened that day at the prison, as well as LEFT OUT IN THE RAIN!

The words of Ephesians 6:10-17 came to life for me that day:

> Finally, be strong in the Lord and in HIS mighty power. Put on the full armor of God so that you can take your stand against the devil's schemes. For our struggle is not against flesh and blood, but against the rulers, against the authorities, against the powers of this dark world and against the

spiritual forces of evil in the heavenly realms.
Therefore put on the full armor of God, so that
when the day of evil comes, you may be able to
stand your ground, and after you have done
everything, to stand. Stand firm then, with the belt
of truth buckled around your waist, with the
breastplate of righteousness in place, and with
your feet fitted with the readiness that comes from
the gospel of peace. In addition to all this, take up
the shield of faith, with which you can extinguish
all the flaming arrows of the evil one. Take the
helmet of salvation and the SWORD OF THE SPIRIT
WHICH IS THE WORD OF GOD. (New International
Version)

I wasn't just in a battle; I was in a war—for my marriage and family!

If I was going to win this battle, the first thing I needed was God's unlimited mighty power! My own strength, sufficient though it seemed, would not be enough to sustain me. Secondly, I needed *the armor of God* to be able to *stand my ground*, and the *shield of faith* to be able to *deflect the arrows of the evil one*. Finally, and most importantly, I needed to become an expert with the *sword of the Spirit* (the word of God) because the battle I was fighting was a spiritual one.

That day, I made a commitment to my Commanding Officer to enlist in His army and become a skilled soldier. I believed this commitment was going to take disciplined devotion to the word of God and a tenacity that would not quit, no matter how hard the struggle.   Yes, I would face adversity, but I was up for the challenge! *"Ha haaa!"* I chuckled, *"All the enemy did was stir me to action!"* In fact, I was fired up! I spoke out loud, *"Devil, you will not destroy my marriage! You will not tear apart our family! And I will not let you have our future! The victory is ours! In Jesus' Name!"*

Kevin received the news of the incident from the guards and wrote the following letter:

8/23/4

Rachel, Chris and Noelle,

It's 4 pm on Saturday. You should be almost back to Seattle unless you went to Kimberly's. I think I finally have enough composure to write this letter without bawling like a baby. My heart is hurting so bad for all of you. I feel like someone stuck a knife in it. What happened to you today was an atrocity! Several friends said they are not aware of this ever happening in the past, though you can't be the first. I am so very sorry to have put you through such pain and anguish. I prayed immediately for God to encourage you as you drove away. (I never saw you; I think the guards waited until you were gone before they paged me to the front office.)

Shortly after you left I was paged to the office. Three cops plus the lieutenant pulled me into the admin office. All were very angry at me. They told me you had just come to visit. They said you were rude and said some smart-aleck things to them (which I know is completely not true to your character). They said I "had better get it straightened out" and "if she does that again, she'll never be allowed back." I know you're probably angry reading this knowing this is a misinterpretation of the facts. Don't be angry. Just forgive them as I have. It's their job to create a culture of fear. In fact, they freaked me out for a few moments. I thought they were going to put me in the hole which they do if you upset them or talk back to them. Wow! What a mess.

Though my heart ached and tears were dripping down my cheeks today, I thanked God and praised Him anyway. No matter what trials we face, he is God and we need to encourage ourselves in Him just like David did when his family was kidnapped and his men wanted to kill him.

On the upside, one of my friends explained to a different counselor that my phones still hadn't been turned on. This counselor said for me to be at his office at 8:00am on Monday morning and he will give me a couple of phone calls as well as get my visitor list (and hopefully phone list) approved.   So we will be able to talk soon!

So I exhort all of you to be strong in the Lord. Lean totally on Him for strength and encouragement (as I am confident you are doing.) Remember, none of this surprises God. He will use it all for good!

It was still wrong how you were treated today. I'm so sorry that I've put you all in this position. Please hug

Chris and Noelle one more time for me. I miss all of you so much. I long to see you this coming weekend. I pray God will heal your hearts from today. We have to keep humble subservient attitudes with the prison staff.

Love Kevin (Dad)

COMMUNICATION AT LAST

I hadn't received the letter yet but on Monday morning at 8:06, my phone rang. I got a nervous feeling in my gut knowing that this was finally *the* phone call. When I said hello, a pre-recorded voice came on saying, *"This is the Federal Bureau of Prisons. You have a collect call from…*pause… *Kevin McCarthy…*pause… *Are you willing to accept the charges?"* As if the automated voice was listening, I gave a resounding "*Yes!*"

Kevin's strong but emotional voice reached my ears. *"Rachel?"* I don't remember much about our conversation other than Kevin apologizing for what had happened to me at the visitor center, me crying, and the awkwardness of knowing that all telephone conversations were monitored. What an awful feeling, having waited this long to share our most gut-wrenching feelings with one another and yet knowing somebody was listening in!

But we had communicated! That's what mattered. And affection was stirred again in both of our hearts. We were both so grateful the counselor had finally intervened in our situation and allowed Kevin the mercy of a couple phone calls without the official approval and agreed to get the visitor list approved. Kevin and I were already learning some valuable lessons: Take nothing for granted and appreciate every act of kindness! Even his letters seemed to be more precious to me now that communication had been so sparse.

The next letter:

8/23/4

Hi Rach—

1 John 5:4 For whatever is born of God overcomes the world; and this is the victory that overcomes the world-our faith. (New American Standard Bible)

Well, victory is ours! We made it through a strong spiritual battle this weekend! The devil thought he would assault us and discourage us but he only made us stronger! I was so full of joy to get five minutes with you (on the phone) this morning and fifteen minutes tonight. That was awesome.

You should know that you are a real testimony to the men I hang with. Most long to be married and only dream of finding someone as awesome as you. Frank told me that he hopes God will give him a wife just like you. Frank took a 20-year plea! He gets out in three years. His wife divorced him in his sixth year of prison. Frank is just one of the stories I've heard that make my sentence look like nothing. We have much to be thankful for...

"Oh my gosh! I can't even imagine a twenty-year sentence!" I thought. Suddenly I was aware of how important perspective is. I realized I needed to get my eyes off my circumstances and onto God and be thankful! *Thank you God, Kevin didn't get a 20-year sentence*! And although we have had our share of bad news, for every piece of bad news there is at least one piece of good. I choose to dwell on the good! We cannot control what happens to us but we can control how we *respond* to it! That day, I made some vows and wrote them in my journal. The following entry was written on August 19, 2004:

-I will choose to dwell on the good!

-God will be my joy and the joy of the Lord will be my strength!

-I will put all of my trust in Him!

-I will choose to praise His Name, no matter what-simply because He is worthy of praise!

-I will keep my mind on Him and He will keep me in perfect peace. (Isaiah 26:3)

-I will not be anxious about tomorrow, for every day has enough problems of its own.

-Each day I will accomplish God's will for that day.

50

-God will do great and mighty things in and through my life. I don't live in the natural, I live in the supernatural!! (Yes, I really did write that!)

-His strong arm is holding back the tidal wave of debt and I shall NOT be overcome!!

Then I wrote out the following passage:

"Do not fear, for I have redeemed you; I have called you by name; you are Mine! "When you pass through the waters, I will be with you; And through the rivers, they will not overflow you. When you walk through the fire, you will not be scorched, Nor will the flame burn you. For I am the Lord your God, The Holy One of Israel, your Savior…" (Isaiah 43:1b-3a NASB)

Oh how I wish I would've ripped this page out and put it on my wall! Little did I know I would be tested over and over again to keep these words!

THE FIRST VISIT

The visiting room looked like a large cafeteria. There were round tables in a random pattern throughout with odd numbers of plastic chairs pulled up to them, most of them full. On good weather days, the guards would open up a small outdoor patio area with a few tables. Both areas were under the constant surveillance of prison guards who looked more bored than worried about any raucous activity. The level of chatter was high and the spirit was much lighter than the weighty silence of the visitor line in the lobby. If an inmate knew ahead of time that his friends or family were coming, he could stand behind a pane of glass to the left of the line and wait and watch as the visitors filed in and the "cops" called the awaiting inmate.

On this day, August 28, 2004, at approximately 8:30 am, Kevin was waiting anxiously on the other side of all that glass. He looked quite different, head shaved military-style, thinner, and wearing the commissioned green prison uniform and clean, white tennis shoes. Finally the moment came; we made it through the scrutiny of the prevailing guard as well as the computer scan. (I was more than relieved when the guard was not the same one I had cursed out previously.) Chris, Noelle, and I sheepishly made our way into the visiting room.

"KEVIN MCCARTHY TO THE VISITOR CENTER," announced the guard over the loud speaker. But Kevin was already there getting frisked, and we were all hugging each other within seconds. Finally, after what truly seemed like the longest three weeks of our lives, we were together! Under the beady eyes of the guards or not, we were determined to make the best of the next several hours in the sterile Sheridan Visitor Center. No, there were no conjugal visits. In fact, if the embracing goes a little longer than the presiding guard is comfortable with, he will call you out.

But we didn't care about that right now. We hadn't seen each other, so as you could imagine, there was a lot to catch up on. The kids were starting their new schools the following week. Chris would be going to a large junior high. Noelle was continuing on in the private school with my parent's financial help. I was now working full-time for a company where Kevin had previously been employed.

After Kevin heard all about the kids and then me, he began to tell us about his new life in the camp. Before we knew it, 2:50 pm rolled around and a voice over the loud speaker interrupted our exchange, *"VISITATION IS NOW OVER. PLEASE CLEAR THE VISITOR CENTER."* Just like that, our time ended. I hated that sick feeling with which I was all too familiar. We milked every one of those last ten minutes with our multiple good-byes and hugs. Our anniversary was coming and it would be our first one separated from each other. This was our new normal, at least for the next three years and eleven months, minus time off for good behavior.

THROWING THE FIRST STONE

On Sept 3rd, I received the following letter:

8/30/4 Happy Anniversary!! Big 18 for sure. Never thought anyone could love me so long.

Dear Rachel, bride of my youth, youthful bride of my present,

Today is our special day. I am reflecting how beautiful you looked in your white dress on our wedding day. I remember watching eagerly as you made that eternal walk down the aisle. The fun we had shoving cake in our faces. The excitement of getting in the Cadillac, chauffeured by my dad. The anticipation of the evening and the dream-like nights and days on Catalina Island. And best of all- you are more beautiful today inside and out than you were even then. And our love is so much richer. We've weathered some serious storms of life together as we still are doing. But I couldn't ask for a better running mate!

This time apart has allowed me an opportunity to stop and smell the roses as they say. I've been able to think about you and us with a clear head, undistracted by the hectic world.

Well, I hope the kids are doing well. Give my love and lots of hugs and kisses to the kids. I miss them both dearly. I'm proud of all of you.

Oh, I'm reminded of a Nigerian brother here in camp. Putting all things in perspective, Hodgy was arrested smuggling heroin into the country. Like me, he was originally told he would do life in prison. Because he was arrested, he was in jail from the get-go. Two weeks after being told by his attorney he would spend life in prison, his wife of 11 years left him! She immediately quit taking his phone calls from jail. His bail was set at four million, which his family could not raise. He was sentenced to 20 years. He will now get out one year from December. He is one of the nicest Christian guys here. Everyone loves and respects him. He's been in prison since 1989 and has an incredible attitude. I'm almost certain I would not share his attitude if I were doing a 20-year term. His is an amazing and sad story.

All things in perspective-you are an amazing wife and best friend and we have much to be thankful for. I love you, Hon. Keep your faith strong. I'll see you soon and talk with you even sooner.

Love, Me!

PS: My chapel job has been approved and I start tomorrow!

Boy, after reading this I was sad for Hodgy. Though I didn't know him, I truly felt terrible about his plight. From his wife's standpoint, I totally got it! The load of pain and heartache was too much to bear! Could any woman be expected to wait twenty years for a convicted criminal? Life had served her two bleak and dismal paths, both as a result of Hodgy's wrongdoing. Divorce happened to be the less painful route.

My husband, too, was also now a convicted felon! I knew when he got out he would have a felony conviction on his record. He lost his right to vote. It would be difficult to find a job. Yes, I could stack up the offenses I had against him and I would be justified. I could rant about how I was never in agreement with the decision to take the job with HMC! Add to that all the times he had acted independently of me and led us both into a ditch. I could stand up on my soapbox in front of a group of women and get everyone to agree that divorce is the solution! And making the choice that Hodgy's wife made would certainly be heralded. It would definitely remove the constant turmoil I was feeling in the pit of my stomach. I could move on and put all of this in my rearview mirror. The grief and pain would eventually turn to toughness and I would be just fine!

Kevin was right. Throughout the last eighteen years, we had gone through some serious stuff. Our upbringings were pretty much polar opposites. I had come from a background of financial conservatism, religious values, and stability. Chaos was more the norm for the McCarthy's, moving every year to make a better living, and being much more liberal in their financial, as well as moral disciplines. I had realized early in our marriage that Kevin had strong defenses around his heart so he didn't get hurt. It had also been said that he had a will like a bulldog that had gotten a grip and wouldn't let go. I lost many of our arguments simply because he would bully his way through them and I would eventually give in.

Yet I knew that underneath this strong demeanor, as you can conclude from reading from his letters, was a gentle heart. The name Kevin actually means *gentle* and *kind*. Could it be that God was using this prison experience to "crucify" the outer layers of control and defensiveness, and bring forth a more humble, gentle heart underneath? Could it be that this time in the "crucible" was giving him a new perspective in order to see me and the kids through eyes of appreciation and begin to treat us differently? How could I possibly abort a mission that surely God was involved in to get my husband's attention and draw him to his knees?

Furthermore, who was I to get up on a soapbox? Didn't I have my own weaknesses and imperfections? Aren't we all a "work in progress"? (Some of us just take more work than others!) The passage that came to mind was when the Pharisees brought a sinful woman to Jesus...

> The teachers of the law and the Pharisees brought in a woman caught in adultery. They made her stand before the group and said to Jesus, "Teacher, this woman was caught in the act of adultery. In the Law Moses commanded us to stone such women. Now what do you say?" They were using this question as a trap, in order to have a basis for accusing him. But Jesus bent down and started to write on the ground with his finger. When they kept on questioning him, he straightened up and said to them, "If any one of you is without sin, let him be the first to throw a stone at her." Again he stooped down and wrote on the ground. At this, those who heard began to go away one at a time, the older ones first, until only Jesus was left, with the woman still standing there. Jesus straightened up and asked her, "Woman, where are they? Has no one condemned you?" "No one, sir," she said. "Then neither do I condemn you," Jesus declared. "Go

now and leave your life of sin." (John 8:3-11
NIV)

I realized when I read this that after everyone went
away and only Jesus was left, he had every right
according to the law to pick up the stones and stone
the woman. He was the only one without sin. Yet, he
lived by a higher law: the law of mercy and forgiveness.
He had mercy on the woman and forgave her sins
whether she deserved it or not as he said, "*Go now, and leave
your life of sin.*"

Wow! What an example to us all! How can we
condemn each other when we too are full of sin
ourselves? We forgive *because* He first forgave us—
when we didn't deserve forgiveness. Furthermore, if
we do not forgive others, the Bible says that our Father
will not forgive us (Matthew 6:15). If I were to follow
Jesus' way completely, then I needed to allow mercy
and forgiveness to overrule my feelings of intense
anger and resentment.

I journaled and prayed that day that I would be
able to let go and truly forgive Kevin as God had so
graciously forgiven me. His next letter confirmed my
feelings:

9/7/4

Dearest Rachel,

*There is so much to say because we can't be together at the
moment. Though I desire a quick return, I am thankful
for this time. It really is refreshing. Really, how many*

men would long for an opportunity to take an extended sabbatical from a very hectic rat race. I feel privileged in that sense that I can get away to spend time with God. I can get back to my first love-Jesus. I don't want to sound at all insensitive to the burden this places on you. I just thank God that you are passing the burden onto Jesus also. Together, while apart, we'll each become strong in the Lord and in the power of His might.

Try not to be angry with me. Realize that on the surface things sound good, I am in the belly of the great fish because of my disobedience. Unfortunately, like the innocent sailors on Jonah's boat who were frightened by the sudden tempest, you and the kids and others are having to experience this storm too. You certainly didn't deserve it. I don't blame you for getting angry. But do realize that I am becoming the man you have been praying for, for 18 years.

You are so awesome! Man, hun, I just love you sooooo much! You are making wise choices.

I'm excited that your parents are loaning you the money and fixing the car.

I got the money you and my parents sent for my necessities from the prison store. Thank you so much for the sacrifice (to my folk, too).

Please let the kids know they have letters coming this weekend. I got both of their cute and funny cards.

Romans 16:19-20 For the report of your obedience has reached to all; therefore I am rejoicing over you, but I want you to be wise in what is good and innocent in what is evil. The God of peace will soon crush Satan under your feet. (NASB)

I love you babe, Kevin

Many more expressive letters followed:

9/9/4

Hey Rach,

Ephesians 5:25, 28 Husbands, love your wives, just as Christ also loved the church and gave Himself up for her...So husbands also ought to love their own wives as their own bodies. He who loves his own wife loves himself...(NASB)

I love you so much. Knowing you are there loving me and enduring this trial gives me great joy. You are a special woman. Certainly God's chosen mate for me. Any other woman would have tossed me aside years ago. If I can ever say I've accomplished anything in this lifetime it will only be because you have been so faithful to pray for me and love me unconditionally. You are 100%, Pure, bona fide awesome! Thank you for being you.

My love to the kids. Hugs and kisses!

With all my heart, Kev

I wish I could tell you my heart swelled up with reciprocating love for Kevin. But unfortunately, there were far too many burdens, mostly financial, weighing down on me to allow myself the luxury of sentimental thoughts and prose. I was in survival mode, in which needs were reduced down to the very basic: providing for my children and getting out from under a suffocating mountain of debt. And for this to happen, I needed a higher paying job, a paid-off car, and eventually, our own place to live.

I could feel God's presence as He seemed to be keeping me in the eye of the hurricane. I also began to experience His provision. I had been making payments to a private party on a car and I was able, with the help of my parents, to pay off the remaining balance. My car was paid in full! I landed a higher paying job without direct experience as an office assistant at a prestigious dental office in Bellevue. I also started paying off the smaller items on the debt ledger while Kevin wrote letters to the larger creditors. My in-laws weren't charging me but I agreed to give them a small amount every month just to take some responsibility for living with them. I continued to tithe to my church, no matter what. I reasoned that I didn't have enough money for everything anyway! What did I have to lose?

I wrote Kevin a serious letter about getting our finances in order after he was released. I refused to live like we had in the past! We desperately needed to change our ways.   In the letter, I referenced the following scripture:

> But whatever was to my profit I now consider loss for the sake of Christ. What is more, I consider everything a loss compared to the surpassing greatness of knowing Christ Jesus my Lord, for whose sake I have lost all things. I consider them rubbish, that I may gain Christ and be found in him, not having a righteousness of my own that comes from the law, but that which is through faith in Christ-the righteousness that comes from God and is by faith. (Philippians 3:7-9 NIV)

A couple days later I received a reply:

9/13/4

Hi Rach,

I totally concur with you on the handling of our finances differently and living within our means. When I get out of Sheridan, I first have to go to a halfway house, then home. While home I have to check in with my probation officer and he has to get a full financial statement from me, frequently. Whether I want this or not, it will for sure hold me in check.

Things are going well here. I am excited about studying the Word. My goal is to not only know what I believe and why, but also be able to defend my belief through the word. I am starting an in-depth study on spiritual discipline(s) and will teach on them beginning in two weeks. Pray for me.

God is taking care of me in here. I am continually blessed with what are ordinarily little things. But in here they are huge. Like a guy handed me a couple bell peppers and a tomato—wow! Yummy! You'll never understand how huge that blessing is because they are so available outside of here. But in here they don't serve fresh veggies very often. I think these came from a horticulture class garden. I was also given three pairs of sweat pants, two gym shorts, a winter beanie and workout gloves. Oh, and I found some warm slippers someone threw away when they left the camp. They are in decent shape and you can't buy them here. The list goes on... someone even gave me a highlighter-impossible to get normally.

Anyway, like God is supernaturally taking care of you, he is also taking care of me in little ways.

Well, honey, bedtime. I love you. I'll talk to you soon. Can't wait to see you when you come visit Saturday, and give you a big squeeze!

Love you! Kevin

DEATH IN THE CEMETERY

Even though Kevin was serving the sentence ordered him, we had been sending emails and letters back and forth to his lawyer, Carol, about the possibility of an appeal. I was certain that once the appeal was presented, Kevin would be given a "more just and fair" sentence and be home in six months to a year at the very most. We were convinced there had to be some kind of loophole for cases like ours in which the punishment clearly did not reflect the crime. I prayed for a miracle while anxiously awaiting the positive news regarding the appeal from Carol.

But to shatter any glimmer of hope I was desperately grasping, I received instead a sobering email, reaffirming Kevin's 48-month sentence. There would be no appeal. There would be no early release (aside from good behavior). There would be no "miracle."

After receiving the devastating news from Carol, I was so distraught I left the office and drove a short distance to a shady cemetery. I parked my car, slumped down in my seat, and sobbed and sobbed and sobbed some more. I looked out of my car window through my watery eyes and saw the grave sites and knew something inside of me must die as well. *I had to die* to my false hopes of Kevin "miraculously" being released early. *I had to die* to my idea of everything being okay. *I had to die* to the way I wanted all of this to go. I had to accept *God's* will for me, whatever that was. I sobbed even harder at the reality of doing so.

My hopes were completely shattered. My heart was heavy and broken. I felt like somebody had scattered the pieces of my life all over that cemetery. *"It was not supposed to go this way, Lord! You can't let them win!"* I cried some more.

After wrestling through my feelings for quite some time, I was finally able to surrender my will and pray that difficult prayer, *"Not my will, but Yours be done. You know what's best... I will trust your plan."*

I took a deep breath, wiped my wet face and drove away from those scattered tombstones, knowing that part of me was buried there in that cemetery. I wrote the following in my journal:

We get ourselves into trouble when our faith and trust shift from Him alone to a certain circumstance. He is above our earthly circumstances. His ways are unsearchable, higher than ours. We know not what He will do or even when He will do it and how. It is not for us to know these things for then we would not need faith. Our job is only to trust and believe. Child-like faith, and simple trust. "My daddy can do anything" kind of faith. Really, it takes the burden off of us and places it where it should be—on our Burden-bearer. He delights in being God! He loves to rescue His kids!

That same childlike faith was expressed through Noelle when she said, "Daddy will be home when God wants him home."

Rejoice! His timing, though not mine, is impossible to understand or predict. Let it go! Rest, knowing He's got it all worked out. To Noelle I would say, "Daddy's on a long vacation with God! He will return better and stronger than ever... more equipped for the work God has for him and more in love with me and his kids.

So…"Rejoice always; pray without ceasing; in everything give thanks; for this is God's will for you in Christ Jesus." (1 Thessalonians 5:16-18 NASB)

1/13/5

Hi Rach,

Well, I hardly know where to start… Sorry that Carol's email was so discouraging. I feel your pain. My heart is truly heavy for you. This is one of those moments I feel complete helplessness. I can do nothing to comfort you. I can't even be there to give you my shoulder or a big hug. I'm sorry this is the case. On the other hand I can do a lot for you- through Christ who strengthens me (and you). I can pray for you and trust that God will console you. He will be your husband for me. He is your compassionate Father. He is your best friend that sticks closer than a brother. So I pray that you will continue as you always do, to run to your Strong Tower. He will make you glad.

What I find myself doing is concentrating on what God is doing in me and through me <u>at the moment.</u> I don't look or put a date on my release. I know in my heart that when God is done pruning me, He will release me regardless of what we see—no BOP rule or regulation can hold me once God says to release me.

66

In the meantime, I put everything on the altar, everything. My dreams of business, success, my family, all of it is on the altar.

Speaking for myself, I have squandered many years bucking Him. It is now time that He is breaking me of all hidden areas, all resistance, all fears, all idols, everything that keeps me (us) from being 100%, unequivocally His and His alone. It is when we are weak His power is perfected. It is when we are foolish that His wisdom is demonstrated. It is in complete, heart-felt depth of humility that He will exalt us. And if that moment comes we can testify, 'He broke us only to mend us again, He weakened us only to perfect His power through us. He humbled us, only then to exult us.' (Hosea 6:1) And if exalted one can only say "to God be the glory."

Rach, you are my hero. I don't know of any woman with your virtue and grace. You have one of the greatest foundational disciplines anyone could ask for instilled in your character—you are quick to run into the arms of your Father. And for that very reason, I am even confident that by the time you get this letter you will have already tasted great victory over this matter. You know how to run the race to win!

I love you, Kevin

FIRED!

I was thankful for my new dental office job and the increased pay. It didn't take long, however, to realize there was great conflict going on in the office. The office consisted of two dentists, Dr. Robert and Dr. Pam, who shared the same space and staff. The staff was all female and if the office were compared to a food chain, I was on the bottom. At the top were the dentists, then the hygienist, dental assistants, the finance office manager, and then the administrative staff. It became known to me that Dr. Robert had wanted to hire me; Dr. Pam had not. She did not like the fact that even though I had a warm personality and office skills, I had no direct experience in the dental field or in using their specific dental software.

One afternoon, the office was closed to patients while we all assembled for an office meeting. In discussing the ideal way the office should run, Dr. Robert singled me out and said I had been an example of how he wanted to greet his new patients and make them feel welcome and comfortable. I could feel my face turning red as the other women who had joined sides with Dr. Pam glared at me. It seriously would've been better for me if nothing was said at all and I could just continue to do my job.

After that day, things went downhill fast! I felt as if I was under a microscope by the clique who wanted me out. The stress was tearing me apart! As much as I tried to smile and not let it affect me, I made some careless errors and knew they did not go unnoticed. When I got in my car to drive home, I didn't know whether to scream from the pressure or cry because I knew I was hated. Add to that the bumper-to-bumper daily commute heading north on I-5 and the grueling drives to and from Sheridan on the weekends and I was ready to crack!   I wanted to put a bumper sticker on my car that read, "GOOD-BYE CITY, HELLO COUNTRY", and get the heck out of there.

I remember coming home after one of these taxing weeks and throwing my Bible across my bed in my tiny attic room, crying, *"Lord, deliver me! I can't keep living like this! Move me to Oregon! Get me out of here, please!"* My prayers were erratic and even illogical but desperate and heartfelt.

On a Friday afternoon during my third harrowing week, Dr. Robert asked to see me in his office. *"I knew it!"* I thought, *"I could just tell something was going down!"* Everybody was acting so strange and quiet. I got up from the reception counter and followed him into his office. He closed the door behind him and asked me to sit down across from his desk (gulp). He began very quietly by saying he was sorry and that he hated to do what he was about to do. *"There have been some conflicting opinions here in the office and it seems I'm outnumbered."* He had tears in his eyes. He went on, *"I really like you and the joy and spark you've brought to the office, but there are those that don't recognize that. I'm going to have to let you go. And I think it's best that you go ahead and clean out your locker today, and I'll make sure to give you two weeks' pay."*

Wait, what??? I was taken aback. *He was not giving me two weeks' notice; he was firing me, but paying me for the next two weeks!* I was so happy that I wanted to burst! But if he knew what I was thinking, he'd have been completely confused. So I buried my enthusiasm in my chest, assured him I had no hard feelings, and thanked him for giving me the opportunity. Then I walked out to a now vacated office, cleaned out my locker, and skipped out to my car! *Woohoo! I was free! "Thank you, Lord, for delivering me!"* I said aloud.

If ever there was an obvious sign to move, this was it! I basically had two weeks' pay to pack up what belongings the kids and I had left and head to Oregon. *But where was I going? And what was I going to do for a job? A place to live? A down payment?* For some reason, I felt no fear, only the peace of God which truly surpasses all understanding. I trusted God enough to know when He closes a door like He did with my awful job, He will lead me to a better place!

That night when I went to bed I cried out to Him again, "Lord, what should I do? I have to support these kids! And we need to be closer to Kevin!"

The answer came back as clear as a bell. Only it wasn't an answer. It was a question. *"Think about the time that you enjoyed most in your life. What were you doing?"* Immediately I knew the answer. My thoughts went back to living in Arizona when I wasn't sure which preschool to enroll Christopher in, so I decided I would open my own little "school"—in my home! So I spread the word at the church we attended and before I knew it, I had five moms that signed on to the idea of bringing their preschool-age children to me three days a week during the school year. I developed a character-based curriculum with songs, crafts, and scripture memory. It was a great success! The children begged their moms to come to "Miss Rachel's" and at the end of the day I hated to see them go! Both of my children had thrived in this environment.

There was no reason why I couldn't duplicate this idea in the state of Oregon. I just needed a home, a bunch of preschool supplies, and the proper certification. And instead of a part-time preschool situation, I would open an actual full-time childcare which so many working mothers needed. My faith level was high! I was so excited, I could hardly sleep. Finally, an answer in the midst of the whirlwind; it was wind in my sails! I excitedly wrote a quick letter to Kevin with the following verses:

> "I am still confident of this: I will see the goodness of the LORD in the land of the living. Wait for the LORD; be strong and take heart and wait for the LORD." (Psalm 27:13-14 NIV)

> "Forget the former things; do not dwell on the past. See, I am doing a new thing! Now it springs up; do you not perceive it? I am making a way in the desert and streams in the wasteland." (Isaiah 43:18-19 NIV)

A few days later I received his response:

Dear Rach,

I'm encouraged to know you are totally relying on and expecting the goodness of the Lord. This is definitely a big trial for both of us-especially you with your added burdens. I wish I could be there to bail you out. I do know God has us where we need to be. He is grooming us (refining in the fire, more like it) for the next part of our lives.

You're most definitely my hero! Be strong and let your heart take courage. Yes, wait for the Lord! I love you, my love.

Rach-you are my best friend-a friend that sticks closer than a brother. If I had no other friend in the world, I would be happy and content spending the rest of my life with you (and I plan on doing so). I thank God for you always. In our time apart, I have been able to reflect on life and refocus on the things that are most important. My relationship with the Lord is number one of course, but there is nothing or no one more important to me that you. When I come home I will be your knight in shining armor. I won't be the same old selfish self. Even this prison wouldn't let that guy in here. He's gone. It's all about you and others; not all about me. I decrease so He can increase in my life.

Well honey, I'll say goodnight. Keep my bed warm. Soon you'll never be in bed alone again-you'll have me back looking like The Incredible Hulk (except not green, ha) I'll come home a solid rock physically and spiritually.

Love, Kevin

Bitter to Better

A PLACE OF PEACE

In spite of losing my job, I had a new excitement burning in my spirit. On Sunday, I went to church and talked to Carol (yes, another Carol), my pastor's wife, after the service. Several years prior, Carol and her husband had moved to the Seattle area from Corvallis, Oregon, so I thought she may have a recommendation for me. I explained to her my vision about relocating closer to the prison and opening up a childcare business in my home. *"I think you should move to Corvallis,"* Carol said. Now I had graduated from Oregon State University in Corvallis so I just laughed. *I mean, why would I ever want to go back to my old college town?* But she reminded me that it is a quaint little town with some of the same people living there I had known as a college student.

Having warmed up to Carol's advice, I decided we could add Corvallis to the list of possibilities. After all, it was almost exactly one hour from the town of Sheridan. The following weekend, after a visit with Kevin, the kids and I went on an exploratory mission—first to Salem, the capitol, and then to my ol' alma mater. My goal was to find a home that would be conducive to lots of kids and a relatively close distance to the prison. We had a list of all of the available rental properties, so I targeted the more residential part of town. One by one, we drove by the rental homes and placed calls to the property managers. The very last listing read:

FOR RENT: TWO STORY, 3 BEDROOM, FURNISHED COUNTRY HOME ON VINEYARD PROPERTY $1400 PER MONTH

There was no address, just a phone number. I called the number, left a message, and didn't think much more about it. We returned to Kirkland tired and road weary. I praised the kids for being such troopers while joining me in the pioneering spirit.

Without knowing where I was going, I began to pack. On Tuesday, my phone rang. *"Hi, this is Holly. You called to inquire about our home on a vineyard property."* I gasped! I didn't think any responses were coming from our pioneering expedition. *"Oh yes, thank you for returning my call!"* I answered, *"Could you give me some more details about the home?"* Holly informed me it was an old renovated farm house that sat on 250 acres of both farmland and vineyard just north of Corvallis. There was a large barn within walking distance from the home with rental stalls for horses. She went on to tell me if I rented the home I was welcome to enjoy the surrounding land as long as we treated it respectfully.

Two hundred and fifty acres? My mind went back to the bumper sticker I had wanted to put on my car. I took a deep breath and asked the next question, *"Would you be open to me having a childcare business in the home?"* That was a biggie! There was the wear and tear to consider, multiple vehicles driving in and out of the driveway, and liability issues. I followed up the question by telling her I was a single mom trying to get a fresh start for my family. There was a short silence and then Holly said, *"I'll have to discuss that with my husband and get back to you."*

In terms of operating a childcare business, the home sounded like an ideal place. But we needed a miracle for a landlord to approve a single mom opening a daycare business in a $1400 rental house. It seemed absurd! But I knew God had given me the vision in the first place so my heart was filled with confidence. I asked Kevin and several of my close friends for prayer.

Kevin's answer:

5/16/5

Hi Honey,

I am praying that unless God in His wisdom knows some reason you shouldn't get the farmhouse, that you will get it. It's even furnished? That's amazing! I was wondering what you were going to do for furniture. Lord, thank you for speaking to Holly and her husband to support Rachel and our kids with this house. Amen!

Honey, I wish so bad I could help you through this move. I feel terrible that you have to do this without (and because of) me. All I can do is pray which I do. I am so excited that you are moving to Corvallis. It may be the old college town for you but it represents a fresh start for all of us. A smaller community with a less stressful lifestyle sounds awesome. I will be excited to share your home with you when God lets me come home. Are there any old boyfriends living there I need to worry about? Hee hee.

Well, darling, please always remember how much I love you and how God brought us together. He has a plan and purpose for our lives and is simply working out the details.

You're my hero of the faith! Love Kevin

One week later, we were headed down to Corvallis, Oregon, to view our only option for a rental home.

The home was situated almost directly off the main highway running north and south through town, one mile from the last housing development. When we pulled up I honestly couldn't believe my eyes. It was the quintessential white, tall, country home with green shutters, positioned beside a long, gravel lane bordered by three large walnut trees. Behind and to the south of the home was the majority of the acreage with a large barn surrounded by horse fencing, and in the distance there were grapevine-striped hills as far as the eye could see. And the sky...the sky was everywhere! There were no buildings or tall trees blocking the view in any direction. It was breathtaking!

The inside of the home had been renovated, yet still had the original high, airy ceilings and thick crown moldings characteristic of old farm homes. I could easily picture myself setting up a childcare business on the main floor while allowing Christopher and Noelle the privacy of the upstairs for themselves. And with outdoor playtime being a high priority for me when it comes to preschoolers, I was certain this place would be more than sufficient. I began to rejoice, thanking God for the place before receiving an answer from Holly. After all, He's the One in charge!

Yes! It was a huge responsibility and no, it wasn't as cheap as any apartment I could find. But in order to do what I felt I was supposed to do, I would need a home with a yard for the little ones to play. My kids and I drove back to Kirkland with a renewed vigor about life and where it was taking us. It felt like an adventure. A renewed hope was rising inside of me.

During the next couple of weeks, my faith was greatly tested. I didn't hear anything from Holly. The doubts about her allowing a childcare business in her home tried to rattle the peace in my heart. But I was learning how to trust God's word and not waver! I read and journaled some relevant scriptures to encourage my faith.

> Consider it pure joy, my brothers, whenever you face trials of many kinds, because you know that the testing of your faith develops perseverance. Perseverance must finish its work so that you may be mature and complete, not lacking anything. (James 1:2-4 NIV)

As well as:

> In hope against hope he (Abraham) believed...
> Without becoming weak in faith he contemplated

his own body, now as good as dead since he was about a hundred years old, and the deadness of Sarah's womb; yet, **with respect to the promise of God, he did not waver in unbelief but grew strong in faith, giving glory to God, and being fully assured that what God had promised, He was able also to perform.** (Romans 4:18-21 NASB)

After much prayer and standing on what I believed to be the promise of God, the long-awaited phone call finally came. Holly approved us and agreed to meet us at the rental house with a key!

Another letter from Kev:

Hi Honey,

Congratulations on your new home! I am so excited for you and the kids. You are paving the way for our new life, fresh start, together. We are getting ready to embark on the best years of our lives. God has prepared a future and a hope for us. He is continually proving Himself faithful to both of us through this time.

I appreciate your unfailing and unwavering love more than you could know. Thank you for sacrificing everything for me. Thank you for making the move down here to be closer to me. Thank you for laying down your life to raise our kids. Thank you for being you. I love you more than ever.

When we are reunited it will be like we are newlyweds, except we'll have 20 years' experience to know what NOT to do. We have two incredibly awesome kids, young people that add so much to our joy and fulfillment. I can hardly wait to get back to my family.

I pray for God's greatest blessings in your new home, church and city. Soon I will join you all!

Love forever, Kevin (Dad)

HEAVENLY GIFTS

Shortly after I got the approval on the house, I called my friend Carol to share my excitement. After all, she was the one who had suggested Corvallis! *"Are you going to be at church this Sunday?"* she asked me. *"Yes, I'm planning on it. It may be our last service there,"* I answered. That Sunday, the pastor, Carol's husband Bruce, demonstrated the most wonderful display of God's mercy and kindness. He called Chris, Noelle, and me to come to the front for a farewell message and prayer of blessing over us. Following this, he announced they would take up an offering for me to help with the expenses involved in moving. At the end of the service I humbly accepted a great deal of cash from a very gracious congregation of wonderful people! This pastor and his wife were and always will be shining examples of God's love made evident by His people.

The next blessing happened as we were at home packing. My Dad and Mom drove up with a pickup load of children's indoor and outdoor play items, preschool books and other childcare supplies. There were even tri-fold mats for the children's quiet time; they gave me just the amount I needed. Apparently, a woman they knew was retiring her childcare center and when she heard about me opening one, she told them she'd be more than happy to off-load everything to a good cause—for free! I was ecstatic!

From his position in prison, Kevin couldn't help financially, so he gave me permission to sell any of his items, including his beloved scuba gear, to help with the down payment. Fortunately, a friend of ours, Russ, who was a fellow diver, gave me a generous $2500 for everything. Every little bit made a difference! And the "stuff" didn't matter anymore.

My parents offered to help us make the move, so after a full day of loading a moving truck, my parents' pick-up, and my car with my Mom and Dad, my kids, and our dog Carmel, I was Corvallis-bound. We were all exhausted as we finally turned down the long lane to the farmhouse at 2 am.

I felt in my heart that all the help and financial gifts were a confirmation that we were headed in the right direction. I had a peace in my heart knowing that Jesus was leading the way, providing everything we needed to make the next chapter of our family's life a success. Sadly, however, it was Fathers' Day weekend and we would be moving into this next chapter without the kids' father. The move was bittersweet.

6-19-5 Happy Father's Day to me… (grin)

Hi Rach,

What a weekend huh? How are you feeling? I'll bet you'll be glad to get completely unpacked and all moved in. How long is your mom staying? I need to thank them for all their help.

I am so excited that you are "here". You feel so close. It's weird. Even though we are still limited in our ability to be together, the fact that you now live in Corvallis simply feels like you are close to me. It's a great feeling. I look forward to some surprise visits. And to seeing you and the kids more often. I hope you never get tired of the 50 minute drive. Maybe you'll find some shortcuts?

I am also excited that Russ gave you $2500. It is a direct answer to my prayers. I asked that you would have all the money you needed for the move and for July's bills. I also asked that the things you sell would yield top dollar.

I'm wondering if you are seeing the lightning right now? In the western sky is a beautiful sunset. To the east of us is a lightning storm. Pretty cool. We have way prettier sunsets being so close to the ocean than we did in Seattle.

Well honey, I look forward to seeing you tomorrow night. I need to see you. I miss you so much—especially when there is a sunset we could be sharing.

I love you, Kev

LITTLE LAMBS

I asked Chris and Noelle if they could think of any catchy names for the childcare business. Noelle came up with Little Lambs which was perfect since we were on a farm-like property and because the name Rachel actually means "*Lamb*".

After getting all of the proper childcare licensing and paperwork completed for the State of Oregon, setting up an attractive children's area in my home, and strategically placing my DIY black and white sandwich board sign to alert passers-by, I was ready for business! As a single caregiver, the licensing allowed me to have six children in my care at one time. I was aware that infants and toddlers could potentially take the majority of my attention and energy. So my goal was to accept three to five-year-olds so I could incorporate the curriculum along with many of the crafts and activities I had created in Arizona. Fortunately, there was a local organization which helped connect parents to a registered childcare provider near them which had openings.

My phone began to ring. "Little Lambs Childcare, this is Rachel," I answered with excitement. "Hi, Rachel. Do you have any openings for a three-month old?" A woman asked. "No, I'm sorry, I am only accepting preschool age children at this time," I replied, which abruptly ended the conversation. And then another, "Hi, this is so and so. Can you take a five-month old?" Then another, "Hello, I'm just going back to work and am looking for care for my baby who's eight weeks." Goodness, gracious, I thought, where are all the three- to five-year-olds? I just wasn't set up with cribs and such for babies. Sadly, I would turn the needy mothers away. Days and weeks went by and the small savings I had was running dangerously low. Soon I would not be able to cover the rent. Then my sign was stolen.

"Lord," I prayed, "I know you told me to do this! And I know you wouldn't have told me to do this and then not come through for me!" A couple weeks prior I had thought I heard His gentle words as He gave me the catchy phrase, "Prepare the boat and I'll make it float." Ok, so what else can I do to prepare? I thought. But no answer came. This time I heard nothing. I looked disappointedly around at my perfectly tidy play area and clean floors. Doubting thoughts started to flood my mind. Maybe I'm too far away from town. Maybe I need to take babies. My parents also became doubtful. "Maybe you ought to just go get a job," they said.

The pressures grew heavier. Over the course of the next couple of months, I accepted a couple of preschoolers: one with serious behavioral challenges with a high maintenance mother, and another whose gruff father told me he didn't want his little girl playing outside! The sad part of that equation is that she loved our outdoor time, probably because she had never experienced it!

To add to the struggles, Chris was having terrible allergies from the grass seed and hay farming all around us, and Noelle was discouraged because she hadn't made any friends and she was missing her previous ones from Washington. Both of them were upset at me for moving to Oregon! As a result, they were each acting out in different ways. Chris was getting a D in one of his classes and nothing I said seemed to matter. I took Noelle to buy shoes for a banquet she was attending and she smarted off to me when I gave her my input. Now this may seem like normal pre-teen and teen behavior but I had never known them to act out like this. I felt like a failure as a parent.

The more things pressed down upon me, the more resentment I felt towards Kevin. And as the feelings of resentment grew, the angrier I became. And the angrier I became, the less joy and peace I had in my heart and soul. It was a domino effect that mounted and mounted until one day I took it out on Carmel— just like the proverbial "kick the dog" kind of thing! She was completely out of her boundaries, running after the (well-behaved) landlord's dogs, while barking continuously! I tried yelling loudly at her to stop and she wouldn't obey me. I was furious! I ran after her, grabbed her by the collar, and spanked her several times—hard! Afterwards I thought, *"Oh my gosh! What have I done? She's just being a dog!"* I felt so awful that I cried as I apologized to her over and over again.

Releasing my deepest, most bitter feelings to the Lord became a daily ritual. My friend, Kimberly, had given me a daily devotional book called *Streams in the Desert* by L.B. Cowman. Appropriate title, alright! This female author was all about suffering. And she knew how to give her feelings to God and depend entirely on His strength and word. I began to inhale the words in her book; they became my daily breath and life. Here is an excerpt from the devotional:

> Shall I not drink the cup the Father has given me? (John 18:11b NIV)

To "drink the cup" was a greater thing than calming the seas or raising the dead. The prophets and apostles could do amazing miracles, but they did not always do the will of God... Doing God's will and thus experiencing suffering is still the highest form of faith, and the most glorious Christian achievement. Having your brightest aspirations as a young person forever crushed; bearing burdens daily that are always difficult, and not seeing relief; finding yourself worn down by poverty while simply desiring to do good for others and provide a comfortable living for those you love; being alone, separated from all those you love, to face the trauma of life alone; yet in all these, still being able to say through such a difficult school of discipline, "Shall I not drink the cup the Father has given me?"—**this is faith at its highest and spiritual success at its crowning point.**

She goes on...

In order to have a sympathetic God, we must have a suffering Savior, for true sympathy comes from understanding another person's hurt by suffering the same affliction. We can only help those who suffer by going through suffering of our own.

The most comforting of David's psalms were squeezed from his life in his time of suffering, and if Paul had not been given "a thorn in the flesh" (2 Corinthians 12:7), we would have missed much of the heartbeat of tenderness that resonates through so many of his letters.

If you have surrendered yourself to Christ, your present circumstances that seem to be pressing so hard against you are the perfect tool in the Father's hand to chisel you into shape for eternity. So trust Him and never push away the instrument He is using OR YOU WILL MISS THE RESULT OF HIS WORK IN YOUR LIFE!! (My own exclamation points added.)

WHOA! I could swear L.B. Cowman, a person I have never met, was hiding somewhere in my house, reading my mail, and knew exactly what devotional to write that day for me! Her messages were not only challenging, but transforming! This book helped me to think in a whole new way: I could either resent the suffering and push the "cup" away or I could accept and embrace it, knowing that suffering, though difficult at the time, was forging God's character and love on the inside of me, making me more compassionate and caring towards others who suffer as well. I was committed to the latter.

There are some mountains in our life that we cannot simply climb over or go around in an attempt to avoid. But we must journey THROUGH the valleys surrounding them where the dark shadows lie and the days are dark, lonely, and dreary. But thanks be to our God who is God of the valleys as well as the mount! It is there that the Good Shepherd will lead us to cool streams of water for us to drink and allow his protective rod and guiding staff to comfort us.

Hi Rach,

Sorry you had such a rough day today. I wish I could be there to set things straight with Chris and Noelle. At least we are close enough that we can see each other more often.

I'm very sorry that I have put you in the situation of raising two teenagers. Is there really any good age for a mom to raise kids without the help of the dad? I'll forever look at single moms in a whole new way—with great compassion.

All in all, Chris and Noelle are great kids. They do have their issues, but you are a great mom who will, by God's grace, be able to train them up in all areas. I'm trying to get more dialogue going with Chris too. He wrote me a great letter and I'm writing him back tonight.

I'm still praying that you fill up the house with kids so you don't have to seek other alternatives. It seems like you are so close on the one hand. But it must seem so frustrating as you look at the actual bank balance and only see $400 available for rent. You are handling this so well. I am so blessed to have a woman like you. So many women would be angry and bitter and hard to live with. You are incredible- a true woman of God. Thank *you for continually forgiving me. I am sorry you had to be dragged into my trials.*

I pray that God gives you abundant wisdom, keeps you and the kids safe from harm and the enemy. I also pray for more little kids, that the Lord would confirm His calling you to the biz. And for your joy to return.

Rach, I know it is hard, but make time to get with God. He has always been your first love and the complete source of your joy. He will renew your strength. You are a warrior. Keep fighting!

I love you and I'm proud of you—Kevin

I was making such a pittance with my business that I was finally forced to get help from the Oregon Department of Human Services (DHS). It was shameful! The first time I stood in line, I got about halfway to the counter, turned around, and left! *I can't do this! I have too much dignity!* The enormity of covering the rent and providing for two teenagers was weighing down heavily upon me. I was collapsing under the pressure. As I drove home from DHS, tears filled my eyes as I cried those familiar words, *"Lord, please, just take me! Take my life! I don't want to live anymore! I can't do this!!"*

Fortunately, God did not grant my request. Instead I was left with a choice. I either had to humble myself and ask for help from the State, or admit to Holly I would not have next month's rent. Just the thought of this gave me a queasiness down inside! I had never reneged on a commitment like this before and I wasn't about to go that route. Besides that, she and her husband had been so gracious and trusting to allow me to rent the house. I couldn't let them down!

The next day, I drove back to the DHS office and sucked it up. The clerk looked at my current income status and approved us for $450 per month in the form of a food card. I should've been happy, but it felt like more of a defeat than a victory. Thank God for the minds of innocent children, because when I told the kids, Chris asked if we could spend it on movie theater popcorn and Noelle asked if we could spend it on Starbucks! I laughed.

But I still had next month's rent to pay—due on the fifth of every month. So I reluctantly made a call to the pastor of my church about the shortfall for the rent and he was more than willing to help. Once again, a generous congregation took up an offering for a needy, single mom and her two children. Being on the receiving end was one of the hardest things for me! I had never been on the needy side of the fence and I couldn't wait to be back on the giving side. *At least I can understand a little better how people feel that live this way,* I thought.

It was good to know Kevin empathized with me in his letter:

Hi Darling,

What a rough week for both of us—mostly you. I am so sorry this is so painful for you. If I could turn back the clock (knowing what I now know) I would do it in a New York minute. I hurt when you hurt. My heart is breaking for you. It's nearly impossible to imagine the joy of my life-and so many others-wanting to be dead. You have given hope to so many people for so long and now you feel hopeless.

Hang in there. Keep the faith! And be diligent. (2 Peter 1:5) Once your reputation gets around you will have a waiting list and an abundance of money. You are a kid-magnet. Kids love you and as you've said, "cling to you when the parents come." So rest assured- you will be successful at this endeavor.

So be bold and strong, for the Lord your God is with you. I wish I could be there. But what I can do is tell you how much I love you. And most importantly, I can and do pray for you each and every day.

Love, Kevin

LILIES OF THE FIELD

One morning, as I looked out my window at the dark storm clouds and the fields around my house, I saw patches of lilies that had come up and were now blooming in a beautiful, creamy shade of white. All of a sudden it began to rain—*hard*. The rain turned into hail! Now here were these tender lilies, and I watched as they were getting clobbered! After the storm cloud passed over, I ran outside to look at them, thinking surely they would be in shreds. But they weren't! In fact, they were completely whole, standing tall and majestic as ever. I was shocked! When I came back to the house to read my Bible, I searched for the following passage:

> I remember my affliction and my wandering, the bitterness and the gall. I well remember them, and my soul is downcast within me. Yet this I call to mind and therefore I have hope: **Because of the LORD's great love we are not consumed, for his compassions never fail**. They are new every morning; great is your faithfulness. I say to myself, "The LORD is my portion; therefore I will wait for him." (Lamentations 3:19-24 NIV)

Something happened inside me at that moment! I realized I had been like those lilies. Heavy showers, even hail, had been pounding against me. I was pretty much a basket case, as they say. But after I saw the lilies in their near-perfect state, I knew God's faithful love would sustain us and because of His wonderful mercy, I would *not* fail. I began to cry out, "*Lord, I don't care what happens in my business! I don't care what happens to my house and my finances! I'm going to love you no matter what! I'M GOING TO LOVE YOU NO MATTER WHAT!!*" I had hot tears streaming down my face; my body was shaking uncontrollably. It was a very powerful moment!

I wrote the following in my journal:

> Though at times the burdens bear down hard on

our lives, His mercy will sustain us. Because of His love we can "pop back up." And though it seems impossible even for the dainty flower to bare up under such rain and hail, not even a petal was lost! Even as the flowers keep their faces turned upward, so too, must we keep our faces fixed on Him - the God of all mercies and comfort. He is faithful! I will wait for Him!

From that day forward, it began to rain…a different kind of rain. Provision like I had never known before began to pour out all over me. The phone was ringing daily, this time for preschoolers, two of them siblings, then another, and then another. The interviews with the parents went well and I had four full-time contracts! The over-protective father and his daughter left. The boy with the behavioral challenges and his high-maintenance mom left. I had only two more openings to fill.

I grabbed a few of the light blue Little Lambs flyers I had printed and went across the road to a Nazarene church. I nervously walked in and met the secretary. Her name was Beth. I introduced myself and told her what I was doing and then handed her a flyer. She looked up and said, *"As a matter of fact, I have a foster boy that I need care for. He's been through some rough situations. He's three and his name is John."*

John became the first of two brothers in her care who would join the Little Lambs. The connection I made with Beth turned into a lasting friendship.

A short time after acclimating to five preschoolers, I was walking my pack of youngsters around the property and one of the horse owners from the barn on our property came over to chat with me. Her name was Tabitha and she was pushing her eight-month-old baby in a stroller. *"Hey, do you think you could take Kale while I do horse training here at the barn? Just a few days a week?"* She asked. Wow! Here I was standing in front of this lovely lady and her little guy with beautiful, big eyes and the cutest smile. How could I say no? So regardless of his size, Kale became number six. (Kale became the first of three brothers who would later join our bunch.) I was full!

When I was young, my Mom used to say, *"When it rains it pours!"* And that saying was definitely applicable. My financial picture changed drastically.   My income quadrupled! In fact, I was able to get off of the state assistance and finally experience some relief. From that point forward, I was able to pay my rent without the struggle! I even had a small savings.

My kids were getting acclimated in their new school, making friends, and doing quite well.   My daughter made a friend with the gal next door with whom she could hang out when she wasn't in school. One of the benefits of the relationship is that they were a camping family with an RV and they would invite Noelle to go with them on their camping weekends to the Oregon coast. Any single mom would jump at this opportunity as I did, knowing it was something I could not do for my kids at this time.

On February 14th, 2006 I received another piece of mail from Kevin. This time it was a card:

Rachel, my dearest Valentine. The love of my life!

Being able to send you this card is nothing short of a miracle. Someone handed me several old cards that are no longer available. This Valentine card was among them. God is so good. Even in the little things.

I wish so much I could give you a tight hug and be your comfort today. Instead, I will share the vision I had of us:

Just when I went to grab your hand for a dance I got a tap on my shoulder. Jesus said He was cutting in on our dance. So I had to step aside and let Him take over. As He began to waltz with you, He turned back to me and winked. Then he gently whispered with such comfort and security, "Don't fear. I'll take care of her. You can have the next dance." He grabbed your hand, took you in His embrace and whisked you off your feet as He began swinging you all over the dance floor. The whole room was astonished. Every one cleared the floor and just stood by and watched you dance with Jesus. As the pace picks up, you get a little scared so Jesus just pulls you closer and holds you tighter. You feel greater security in the strength of His arms. As you look into His eyes, His light pierces your soul. All dark, hidden areas yield to His light. I am just waiting patiently on the sideline for my turn to dance. But I have a peace knowing you're in the Father's arms. When He took you from my arms He somehow planted a confidence in me as if to say, "no harm will come to her—she's dancing with the King of all Kings who will protect her as a valiant, mighty warrior."

*So my love, for the moment, God has this dance. Enjoy
Him, learn from Him; let His light radiate through you.
Soon we'll dance together again. Somehow I see Him
dancing with us both from that point on, like a cord of
three strands. I love you more than even words can
describe.*

Kevin

THE MAN IN THE VINEYARD

No matter how much affection Kevin expressed
towards me, I always had a pang in the bottom of my
heart. Although I visited every other weekend and
received a letter from him almost daily, he was not
there *in the trenches* with me. He was not there for Chris
and Noelle's school sports and events, or the daily
grind of their homework. He was not there for church
services, dinner invitations, or just hanging out with
friends. He was not there to share holidays, holiday
parties, or family gatherings. He was not there for the
things couples usually take for granted, like eating
dinner out, a shared sunset, or just a hand-in-hand walk
down a familiar street.

I found out during this period of singlehood that
true loneliness didn't happen for me when I was alone.
It happened when there were many people around who
all had significant others and I was there, alone, in the
midst of them.   I'm sure some of the people in my

sphere of influence had their suspicions of where my husband was but the subject was the elephant in the room that most just tip-toed around. This only made my aloneness more conspicuous. It had been over a year since Kevin had been gone and it would be over two more before he returned. My heart longed for adult companionship.

Enter Justin. He was this "new guy" on the farm property whom the landlords had hired to manage the vineyard laborers. His job was to make sure the vines were properly pruned, cared for, and yielded a high quality of grapes before being sold and hauled off for the production of Willamette Valley wines.

Now when Justin drove up in his white work truck, if I were in the vicinity, he would always stop and talk to me, whether I had the preschoolers with me or not. Much to my own surprise, I was taken aback by his handsome appearance, rugged hands, and body. *I mean, this guy was hot!* And I got the feeling he had some attraction for me as well. Though we never made it past superficial conversation, it was obvious we each had a certain curiosity about the other.

One day as I was walking my tribe of kids through a big field along the edge of the vineyard, I noticed Justin's white pickup parked on the gravel road leading up to the top of the hill. As we got closer, I noticed he was sitting in the truck. I could feel the butterflies, the kind you get when you're a teenager, down in my stomach whirling around. I was about ready to come face to face with him. I looked into the window of the truck but instead of seeing his face, I saw another face! In my mind's eye, it was the face of Jesus looking back at me with a huge smile on His face. *"I'm all you need,"* I heard in my spirit, *"I'm all you need!"*

Whoa!!! What just happened? Sometimes God works in mysterious ways and this was one of those times, because there is really no way to intelligently explain this. It was as if God had superimposed Jesus' face in place of Justin's. And when I saw that face—even for a brief second—it was so full of love and affection, *for me*! I got the message. Loud and clear! He wanted me to be ALL His! And *He* wanted to be all I needed. As Kevin had relayed the vision in the Valentine Card for me, *this dance was to be with Him and Him alone.*

My mind went back to the college campus where I had first become a believer. I remember the young preacher at the campus meeting challenging the college crowd while he said loudly, *"He's either Lord of all (in your life) or He's not Lord at all!"* He went on to say, *"If you're at the altar getting married and you tell your soon-to-be bride or bridegroom that they can have you 364 days a year but the other day you will have another lover, do you think they will take you as their husband or wife? No! You either commit ALL of yourself or NONE of yourself to the other. There is no middle ground."* I can recite it like it was yesterday. These words pierced me to the heart because I knew I had to give 100 percent of my life to Christ and hold nothing back! And that meant staying true to my husband as well.

From that day forward, I was intentional about not giving Justin, (or any other man, for that matter) any undue attention. And ironically, shortly after that, Justin told me he was moving to eastern Oregon! I was sure this had been a ploy of the enemy to strike me at my weakness. God had kept me from heading down a very destructive path. He, most certainly, was answering Kevin's prayers for me.

I wrote this scripture in my journal:

> To him who is able to keep you from falling and to present you before his glorious presence without fault and with great joy- to the only God our Savior be glory, majesty, power and authority, through Jesus Christ our Lord, before all ages, now and forevermore! Amen.
> (Jude 1:24-25 NIV)

I was even more relieved when I read the following letter from Kevin:

Hi Honey,

As I reflect on our marriage—and more importantly, on you—I would not trade our marriage for any marriage in the world. We've gone through plenty of trials together, and I believe we are better people for it.

You are not only beautiful in looks, but also in spirit. I am blessed beyond my wildest imaginations. Thank you for saying "I do" and for holding true to your vows. You have loved me when I didn't deserve it—what a picture of Christ you are! I look forward to the rest of our lives together. I pray we are granted many more years. (Note from me: I know this was and is only by the grace of God)

I love you, Kevin

GOD'S OCEAN OF GRACE

Even though Little Lambs was flourishing and our basic financial needs were being met, I was having a challenge on a different level. One of the characteristics of a childcare business is that one must be open long hours during the day to accommodate the working parents' shift. Some of the local businesses I had researched were open from 6am to 6pm! Now I knew that I could not single-handedly keep those hours, still be a mom, and maintain my sanity, so I settled with the hours 7:15 am to 5:30 pm to accommodate most schedules. Yet, even with the ten-hour days, I commonly had certain parents who would notoriously drop off their child before 7:15 and pick up after 5:30.

These situations would test my mettle. It took everything within me to be able to smile after a long, hard day while still waiting for a parent after 5:45. Though the parents knew they were charged for the extra time, they didn't seem to realize the mental and physical strain this put on us as a family. My own kids took the brunt of it as I was not always able to attend to their needs, school work, and social events as I would have liked. And when I did, I was usually late and exhausted. This was one of the most difficult challenges emotionally for me since I placed a high value on being an involved parent. *How could I feel good about myself if I were running a successful business, yet absent as a parent?* I was greatly conflicted.

It came to a point where I said, *"Lord, I feel like your grace has just run out."* That is when I got a whole new meaning to 2 Corinthians 12:9-10:

But he said to me, "My grace is sufficient for you, for my power is made perfect in weakness." Therefore I will boast all the more gladly about my weaknesses, so that Christ's power may rest on me. That is why, for Christ's sake, I delight in weaknesses, in insults, in hardships, in persecutions, in difficulties. For when I am weak, then I am strong. (NIV)

"My grace is sufficient for you..." I looked up the word *sufficient* in the Hebrew and it meant simply *"enough"*. For me, this translated that whatever the need, His grace will always be enough! His grace is the empowerment we can rely on to get through any situation. In the time of trial our own resources run dry, but His grace is like an ocean that never runs dry; it keeps pouring and pouring. I had been holding up a cup and asking God to fill it. Yet He was saying, *"Lift up your expectation of my grace and know that it is above and beyond what you can imagine or ask for."*

This poem by Annie Johnson Flint says it best. I printed this out, put it in a small picture frame and set it on my window sill as a constant reminder:

He giveth more grace when burdens grow greater,

He sendeth more strength when the labors increase;

To added affliction He addeth His mercies,

To multiplied trials His multiplied peace.

When we have exhausted our store of endurance,

When our strength has failed ere the day is half done,

When we reach the end of our hoarded resources

Our Father's full giving is only begun.

His love has no limit, His grace has no measure,

His power no boundary known unto men; For out of His infinite riches in Jesus

He giveth and giveth and giveth again.

Annie Johnson Flint

After the exhortation of raising my expectation of grace, I started entertaining the possibility of taking a vacation. We had not been away as a family for any kind of fun or adventure since Kevin had gone to prison. We desperately needed some time as a family, to get away from the responsibilities of life, to refresh and reset, *even if just for a week*. But honestly, there was no way I could afford plane tickets, let alone a hotel for the three of us. Furthermore, being self-employed meant I did not get paid vacation other than time off for holidays stated in my contract. I decided to be bold and pray in faith that God would do something miraculous. I was ready to tap into that ocean.

My brother and sister-in-law had recently moved to a suburb of San Antonio, Texas, and had just settled in to a new home. I decided to call my brother, Matt, and ask if we could come down for a visit. I was hoping he would invite us to stay with him at his home.

I walked up to the top of the vineyard with our dog, Carmel, after a work day and called Matt on my cell. I relayed to him the idea of getting away for a while and possibly coming to visit him and his family. Matt was ecstatic. *"Rach, this is the perfect place for a vacation!"* he said enthusiastically. *"San Antonio has everything: Sea World, large waterparks, the River Walk, Alamo exhibit, the caves… There's so much to do here! And you guys can stay with us; we have extra bedrooms!"* Whew! I was so glad he made that suggestion! He continued, *"Southwest is having a $99 one-way sale, anywhere they fly, and they fly to San Antonio."* I excitedly thanked him for the offer, hung up, and did the math.

I could squeeze a measly $500 out of our budget for everything. With the extra fees, the plane tickets alone would run almost $750. We would still need money for food and activities. I wasn't sure how this was going to work. As I started booking the flights, I heard the Spirit's gentle voice say, *"Don't worry about the cost, just trust Me."*

A couple of days later, I received an envelope in the mail from my parents, which was not that uncommon. They quite frequently sent Noelle, Chris, or me encouraging notes and cards. I opened the letter and began to read:

Dear Rachel, Christopher and Noelle,

We were telling one of our friends from church about your situation and they said they felt so bad for you guys that they wanted to send you some money. They are aware that you don't know them but they wanted to do this because they know us and you are our family. Please use this money on whatever you need.

I opened the folded check and it was for $500—made out to me! Woohoo!! This was our vacation money! And I had never even heard of these people! To this day, I don't even remember their names. *"Thank you, Lord! You are so good!"* I said excitedly as if He were standing there. Because I knew He was!

Spring break was coming and I figured our time away would work best then, while the kids had a break from school. So I sent a group message to all of my daycare parents to ask for their permission and each one kindly obliged to take their vacation at the same time. There was no opposition whatsoever!

This time my tears were tears of joy! I felt so incredibly blessed! I couldn't wait to tell Chris and Noelle the news as well as make all the arrangements for the vacation. It was really going to happen. And I knew without a doubt, God had *made* it happen—out of His gigantic storehouse of grace!

Our vacation to San Antonio ended up being one of the most special times we had among the three of us and my brother's family. My generous brother and sister-in-law ended up paying for the not-so-inexpensive tickets to Sea World San Antonio as well as the nearby waterpark. We also visited the famous bridge in Austin where thousands of people come to watch the scores and scores of bats fly out from under the bridge to feed at sunset every night. It was spectacular! Finally, the week ended with the kids and me going to a cave in the Texas Hill Country called the Cave Without a Name, eighty feet underground. Fascinating!

Memories are something nobody can take away from you, and we had made some great ones! I could return to our house in the country knowing that in the midst of the hard times, the Lord had given us a reprieve, a special time away from the pressures, just to enjoy life! What a good, good Father! I returned home with my heart overflowing with joy and gratitude.

THE FINISH LINE

We made it to the "one more year" mark! With all of his Bible study and teaching, Kevin was flourishing in prison (as much as a person can flourish while incarcerated). He was taking piano lessons, becoming a skilled pool player, and even writing a book. Chris was becoming a young adult. He was taking on more responsibilities, and learning how to drive. Noelle was becoming a young lady, excelling in school with honors classes. They had gotten jobs shoveling out horse stalls at a large barn across the street for an hour a day. This took some of the burden off of me for the constant little things for which teens need money.

The intensity of the battle was not much less for me but I was becoming a more skilled warrior in my coping mechanisms. I was learning to be fully dependent on God's grace and strength to get me through each day, sometimes through each moment.

In fact, during this time I referred to myself, unashamedly, as a co-dependent. I knew without a shadow of a doubt I could never have made it through most days without divine intervention.

But, like a long-distance runner, I still needed the perseverance to make it across the finish line which was not visible from where I was. In fact, the thought of Kevin coming home had become more of a fantasy than reality. Most of my Corvallis friends and acquaintances had never met him or even knew he existed.

I came across a piece of history about Florence Chadwick, a woman known for swimming the English Channel. In 1950, on her second attempt, she broke the record that Gertrude Ederle had set for swimming the channel. In 1952, she attempted to swim the twenty-six miles from Catalina Island to the California coastline.

While swimming, she was flanked by attendants in boats who watched for sharks and could pull her out if needed. After fifteen hours, a thick fog set in and Florence began to doubt her ability to complete her course. She swam for another hour, finally asking to be pulled out, as she was *unable to see the coastline due to the fog*. As she sat in the boat, she found out that she had stopped swimming just ONE mile from her destination! (There were no instruments to calculate the distance at that time.)

Two months later, she made another attempt. The same thick fog rolled in but she succeeded in reaching Catalina. She said she kept a mental image of the shoreline in her mind while she swam. Florence Chadwick is now in the Swimming Hall of Fame!

This story really spoke to me. It seemed as if I had been fighting hard to stay afloat for a long time. I had encountered some sharks too. My inner strength and confidence had grown, but the fog was preventing me from seeing the "finish line," and I was ready to be pulled into the boat. Everything within me cried out for this trial to be over! I was, as they say, "done already."

But I loved the way Florence had conquered the fog during her second attempt. *She kept a mental image of the shoreline in her mind while she swam!* She must have been cold, hungry, completely exhausted, and ready to be pulled out of the water. She had been swimming for more than 15 hours! But she hadn't *finished* yet, and it was *fixing her mind* on what was ahead of her that compelled her forward!

A few days after reading about Florence Chadwick, I was talking to my neighbor, Damon. Damon was telling me about the exciting opportunity he had to ride in a small Cessna plane from our farm property (where there was a small airstrip) to the coastline—55 miles or a one-hour drive by car. *"It was amazing how fast it went, Rachel!"* He said, *"We flew up and over the valley and in about fifteen minutes. I could see the ocean!"*

That's it! I thought. Vision! When Damon was lifted up in a plane over the valley, he could see the ocean! I knew that God could "lift me up" over the proverbial fog I was in, and help me "see" my own finish line. I thought about the scripture that says *we walk by faith and not by sight.* I had to remind myself that even though I couldn't imagine Kevin actually coming home, there was soon to be revealed a release date that would serve as our finish line. Kevin *would* be HOME. We *would* be reunited, in our marriage and in our family. I closed my eyes and tried hard to envision his return. I couldn't give up now as we were only "one mile from the shore!"

I wrote the following in my journal:

> Hebrews 12:1-3
>
> Therefore, since we are surrounded by such a great cloud of witnesses, let us throw off everything that hinders and the sin that so easily entangles, and let us run with perseverance the race marked out for us. Let us fix our eyes on Jesus, the author and perfecter of our faith, who for the joy set before him endured the cross, scorning its shame, and sat down at the right hand of the throne of God. Consider him who endured such opposition from sinful men, so that you will not grow weary and lose heart. (NIV)

The next day brought another letter:

Hi Honey,

I'm really tired tonight and my body aches from all the carrying we've had to do in the field. So I will keep this short.

I want you to know I am very proud of how you are handling our separation. You have risen to the occasion. Your faith has increased. Your endurance has increased. You have become a stronger woman all around. You are a mighty woman of valor.

Thank you for being my lover and friend and for being an incredible mother to our wonderful children. You are without a doubt a Proverbs 31 woman.

Hang in there. Take it one day at a time. Praise God for how busy you are. The busier the days, the faster they go. Next year will be here before we know it.

I love you—Kevin

RELEASE DATE

Kevin's release date was based on several factors; good behavior was one of them. Another was his attendance in a 500-hour Cognitive Behavioral Psychology program known as the Residential Drug Abuse Program (RDAP) for which he voluntarily signed up for to reduce the length of his sentence. Once accepted into the class, the release date could be calculated from his completion. Finally, we received a concrete release date (although nothing in the prison system is really concrete), of May 1, 2007.

As the last months unfolded, I started picturing life as if Kevin were with us. We started calling everything "our last. ...apart," such as *our last* Thanksgiving apart, *our last* Christmas apart, and *our last* Valentine's day apart. Now that the reality of his return was approaching, some new questions regarding the transition began to flood my mind: *How will the State let me operate a childcare business with a felon in the house? What will I tell my preschoolers' parents? How will they react if they find out he's been in prison?*

There were also nagging questions on a personal level. What if Kevin hasn't changed...I mean truly, deeply at the core level, changed? And how will I know for sure? For over three years now, I had "heard" all of the words, but, what about the actions that speak so much louder? I did not want to set my kids and myself up for disappointment. So I wrote Kevin an honest letter about us. About the pain he had caused me, starting with losing the first home we were going to purchase on Hollywood Hill, to the crumbling of our lives, home, and reputation over the next two years. All because of foolishness! I didn't hold anything back. I figured his response would be a tell-tale sign of whether he was a different, better person, or if he was the same man who entered Sheridan Federal Prison Camp. Yes, either way I loved him; that was not the point. I wanted to know if all these letters were genuine or not! The answer would determine our future.

Less than a week after sharing my concerns, I received *the letter*. I call it *the letter* because it stood out significantly from the rest. This letter was the most vulnerable, repentant, and gut-wrenching expression I had received from Kevin up to that point. It certainly seemed to satisfy many of the hard questions I had, at least temporarily.

1/25/7

Hey Honey,

Thanks for your two letters. Yeah! Snoopy dance! The earlier letter was really deep. Thanks for sharing your heart with me.

I have to say, I got teary-eyed reading your letter, both about the future and the pain of the past. I've heard men mention living a life of no regrets. How does anyone do that? I regret so many things. I've made so many bad choices. Basically, I've been a screw-up all my life. (I must interject here, I do not agree with that statement. Even "many" bad choices did not make Kevin a screw-up!) Yes, many regrets.

But some things I do not regret: meeting Jesus, marrying you, having two awesome kids. I am not full of shame or guilt. God has delivered me, and you, too, have forgiven me (you are one-in- a-million). The person I am today is a result of all the good and bad choices I've made. Romans 8:28 says, "And we know that God causes all things to work together for good to those who love God, to those who are called according to His purpose." I pray all my regrets will be turned into life experiences for the benefit of others.

110

I never realized just how much I was hurting you. I was too self-centered and selfish. It was all about me. My priorities were all screwed up. I suspect for you—the money, the lifestyle, house, etc., was an anesthetic against the pain. I was like the pusher that kept you in the money, to keep you seemingly happy. We were living a very surface-level life…a façade. Sad! Like so many others, I was blind, but NOW I SEE!

I agree with you that the past is the past. We do not need to dwell on it in a negative way. We will use it to help others escape from their own blind spots. It's time to "keep it real" as they say.

Also, we need to fight to keep our priorities constantly intact. I can see how easily I could get off track (with work). I know this is probably the number one concern for you and for me. You and I will just need to set some parameters and I'll need to stick to them. And you have permission to call me on the table if I start slipping (overworking, chasing the elusive dollar, etc.). You can call a counselor immediately if I need to be put in check. Although by God's grace, I think I've learned my lesson. My highest priority will be you and the kids. I believe everything will be okay.

Well, send pics. Hi to the kids and your folks. I miss you bunches.

I love you, Kevin

Soon after reading this letter I had lunch with one of my ol' university friends, Janey Smith, who now lived in Corvallis. Janey had married a seemingly wonderful man, Brandon, who we had both known from the church we all attended back in our college days. Our journeys with our spouses and children were very similar in many ways. She and Brandon had married about two years before us and started having kids shortly before we did. They had a girl, then a boy who was Chris's age, and then they had one more boy a few years later who was very close to Noelle's age. There was one big difference, however: her marriage dissolved before her kids were all out of school.

We reflected on our similarities while we ate, but then I cut to the chase and asked Janey a more serious question. "We both married good men who loved us and promised us the moon. We were both committed spouses that cried out to God, sometimes daily for change in our man's heart and God's will in our families. What was so different between these two men that one stayed the course and the other did not?" Janey thought for a moment and then said, "I believe it boils down to one thing: the will. You can pray and pray until the cows come home, but if a man hardens his heart and won't allow God to deal with him, what can you do?"

I realized as I drove home that day that I was the "lucky" one. By the grace of God, my man *was* willing to do what it took to change…to become a better man. That's it, plain and simple. Kevin had been like a wild mustang who *allowed* the Trainer to wrap a harness around him and guide him into the corral of discipline (in this case- prison). In this "corral," he *chose* humility and self-reflection. He *submitted* to the correction of the prison system and its authorities. (In Kevin's experience, there were plenty of men who did not.) And in order to grow spiritually, he *succumbed* to God's teaching and training through constant study of His word in the prison chapel. All of these *choices* were an act of a *surrendered will.*

The book of Hebrews says it like this:

> Endure hardship as discipline; God is treating you as sons. For what son is not disciplined by his father? If you are not disciplined (and everyone undergoes discipline), then you are illegitimate children and not true sons. Moreover, we have all had human fathers who disciplined us and we respected them for it. How much more **should we submit** to the Father of our spirits and live! Our fathers disciplined us for a little while as they thought best; but God disciplines us for our good, that we may share in his holiness. No discipline seems pleasant at the time, but painful. Later on, however, it produces a harvest of righteousness and peace for those who have been trained by it. (Hebrews 12:7-11 NIV)

Each of us, if we desire to be true sons and daughters of our heavenly Father, must eventually submit to His discipline. (We really all start out as wild mustangs—some are just wilder than others!) Yet, this spiritual training is in our best interest and will certainly reap fulfilling dividends. Kevin and I had both been faced with a choice to accept this narrower, more difficult way. The hope for each of us is that in the process we were allowing a loving God to build His character in us, to mature us, and reveal in us *who* we are created to be as well as *what* we were called to do.

And there's no one other than God Himself who can take all our experiences—the good, the bad and the ugly—and put them all into one big pot and make an amazing stew out of it! Somehow, in His sovereignty, He can take every circumstance and turn it into something good for those who love God. As Kevin wrote in his recent letter, *"All of our wrong choices and regrets can be turned into life experiences for the benefit of others!"*

I knew at this point that I didn't have to wonder any longer if Kevin's transformation was genuine or not. He was indeed a good man who made some bad choices, as we all do at times. But what mattered is that he was taking responsibility for his actions. Isn't that what God desires from all of us—to admit our faults, confess them and learn from the experience? I will say, this is definitely what a woman wants in a man.

We were down to less than a week of time left when I received one of Kevin's last letters:

4/22/7 (Eight days before release to the halfway house)

Hey Lover,

I can hardly express how excited I am getting. By the time you read this, we'll be down to the last of everything. The last Tues, Wed, etc.

I spent the day spring cleaning and getting rid of most of my junk. Feels weird. There is almost nothing in my locker. All my books and papers are going in a box tomorrow. Wow! We made it!

I thought we had a great visit on Saturday. I hope you thought so, too. Maybe the greatest part is it being the last one! Really, seeing and talking with you was great. Thanks for listening to all my thoughts on what I should do for work when I'm out, even though it might have been overwhelming. There are many unknowns for now but I'm sure everything will work out.

I've included a list of stuff to gather. I'll be very flexible- just do what you can. If you don't want to do a drive- thru, just bring some tasty, healthy food. Your call.

Well, honey, you are awesome. Thanks for loving me so much. Your love for me is like Christ's love for me—a mystery. But thank God for both!

I love you, Kev

He followed the letter up with a long list of clothing and toiletry items to put together for the Community Correction Center, referred to as the halfway house. I was literally taking him from the Sheridan Correctional Facility to the halfway facility in Eugene, Oregon. There were no stops allowed other than fast food restaurants or gas, and Kevin was not allowed to get out of the car. Like the voluntary surrender which now seemed so long ago, we were again on the honor system. I was merely the delivery person!

The Road to Redemption

HARD LANDING

In July of 2007, just shy of three years after his voluntary surrender, Kevin was released from the halfway house in Eugene to reunite with our family.

I truly wish I could tell you that after Kevin was reunited with the family, everything was amazing and wonderful! I wish that I could say we lived in perfect harmony, happily ever after. But if I did, I would be lying, and it would read more like the ending of a Hollywood movie or romance novel. What actually happened was quite the opposite.

When Kevin came home, he struggled with finding a job. He had spent hundreds of hours in prison learning about his "thinking errors" and wanted to share those lessons with the world. But he wasn't ready. So a friend of his, who understood Kevin's situation, gave him a sales job. It was a decent job to get his bearings while reconnecting with friends and family. Then the recession of 2008 hit and Kevin was laid off.

It took time for him to figure out what to do next. As you know, every application a person fills out for any job has a yes or no box with the question, *"Have you ever been convicted of a crime?"* Honesty was our policy, so with every application Kevin attached a letter of explanation. We also had to report to the state of Oregon that we now had a felon living in a registered childcare home. Kevin's letter of explanation:

To whom it may concern:

In July, 2004 I pled guilty to conspiracy to commit securities fraud, wire fraud, mail fraud and money laundering as a result of a crime committed by my former employer in Seattle, Washington between 1995 and 2002.

I was hired as an employee for the company in September, 2000, and worked there until January, 2002. I quit just before the company was ordered into receivership.

Prior to any indictments, I accepted a plea bargain and cooperated fully with the federal prosecutors in the prosecution of the owner and 11 other employees. I received a 48-month sentence.

I served my entire sentence in Sheridan Federal Prison Camp from August 9, 2004 until May 1, 2007. I went from Sheridan to the Community Correction Center in Eugene, OR, until July 13th, 2007 when I was released to my wife's residence.

While in Sheridan, I spent numerous hours in

Christian religious study as well as studying thinking errors. I voluntarily attend the 500-hour Residential Drug Abuse Program primarily for all the education I could get on correcting thinking errors.

In summary, I recognize that I was greedy and selfish in my prior thinking. I am cognizant of this weakness and have set up numerous safeguards around me to help me avoid falling back into the same thinking patterns. I am in constant contact with pastors and other friends that I have asked to hold me accountable for my lifestyle choices and behaviors. Thank you in advance for allowing my wife to continue serving the children that have come to love her as a provider.

Regards,

Kevin McCarthy

Fortunately, the State of Oregon DHS allowed me to continue with Little Lambs, and Kevin was able to secure a job working at an auto dealership selling cars. He quickly rose to the top of the sales force and several times he received "Salesman of the Month" award along with a shiny new car to drive. But like any creative entrepreneur, he had a restless spirit and knew that his true purpose and mission was not to sell cars for the rest of his days.

We struggled in our marriage, in our roles and in our communication. We had been separated three and a half years. During this time, my survival instincts had kicked in, and as a result, I had become a much stronger and more independent individual. I had grown accustomed to being on my own and operating as if my life depended on me. As much as I wanted and needed a break, I couldn't just hand the reins of provider over to Kevin.

I had to learn to trust again. And the only way for this to happen was through time and proven character. I really needed Kevin to show me through his actions that he valued Chris, Noelle and me more than anything else in his life, and that we far surpassed any satisfaction a business endeavor could ever bring. Furthermore, I needed to know that the many loving relationships that we had with family and dear friends (so many of which had helped sustain me), were as precious to him and they were to me.

A STRONG FOUNDATION

What we really needed was a fresh start, a new foundation, on which to build our future *together*. Our first "structure" had obviously collapsed, and the adversity over the last several years had caused us to dig down deep, underneath all of the rubble into the hidden places of our heart. We had to examine the pride and selfish ambition that had set us up for such collapse. It is human nature at a time like this to find somebody else to blame. But Kevin and I both knew that we had to take full responsibility for our actions in order to change, and rebuild a structure that *would* withstand the storms of life.

Jesus taught about this subject in the book of Matthew:

> "Therefore everyone who hears these words of mine and puts them into practice is like a wise man who built his house on the rock. The rain came down, the streams rose, and the winds blew and beat against that house; yet it did not fall, because it had its foundation on the rock. But everyone who hears these words of mine and does not put them into practice is like a foolish man who built his house on sand. The rain came down, the streams rose, and the winds blew and beat against that house, and it fell with a great crash." (7:24-27)

Jesus was contrasting two foundations: one built on the rock and one built on the sand. By putting his words into practice we are essentially building our lives on solid ground. Even when the storms of life come and beat against us, (and we can be certain they will beat against us), we will be able to stand strong! Now who, in their right mind would build their house on a sand bar, instead of a solid foundation? Unfortunately, this is what happened to us when it was not God's will for us to join Lawrence in building a fraudulent company. That was surely a sandy cliff which eventually broke off and fell into the ocean!

Thank God we have a loving Father who, if we allow Him to, will help us to get off the shifting sand, give us the tools we need to rebuild, and restore a strong foundation. He'll reveal our weaknesses and help us make them strong and sure.

In a marriage, this fortification takes vigilance on the part of each spouse. We must constantly examine our hearts for errors and cracks that can, over time, cause enough wear and erosion to collapse the whole structure. I believe He desires our marriages to become well-built lighthouses in the storms of life so we can help others steer away from the rocks that cause damage and destruction. Sometimes it takes years for a marriage to have a foundation strong and secure enough on which to build an amazing "structure" together.

It had been years and we weren't there yet. In fact, several years after Kevin was released, some circumstances arose that made it obvious that we were still not done doing damage control on our foundation. From my perspective, it seemed he was falling into the same pitfalls that had trapped him in the first place: focusing solely on a business venture while turning a blind eye and deaf ear to the loving people around him. I had attempted to confront the issue (as he said to do in one of his letters) to no avail.

At the same time, he was feeling as if I was not respecting him, and I was having a hard time doing so. We were at an impasse.

This time, I wasn't going to sit idly by and just pray that it would all come to the surface. I felt I needed to take more serious action. So after being gone for a few days and contemplating what I would say and do, I came home and told Kevin I was separating from him for a while. I told him I felt he wasn't listening to me anymore, and I didn't want to repeat the same cycle that I thought we had overcome! I mentioned that one of the definitions of insanity is *"doing the same thing over and over again, but expecting different results."* I suggested he get some counseling.

Separating from him was one of the most difficult decisions I have ever made. I literally packed up my belongings in my car the same way I had done as a single many years ago, and moved in with my parents. I was resolute. For me this was the ultimate test. I believed Kevin's reaction to me leaving would either make or break everything we had endured together to this point. My ultimatum was for him to get some counseling, and I firmly believed he would either rise up to the challenge or it was over!

One day I received a call from my friend Gwen, who was one of the associate pastors' wives from my church. *"Hey, Gwen,"* I answered. *"Hi Rachel. I called to tell you that Kevin talked to Jerry* (her husband) *and said that he was willing to receive some counseling as long as you went with him."* There was a pause. *"What?"* I was livid! *"No, I'm not going to do this, Gwen. This is not about me; this is about him and his work-aholism!"* Another pause. Finally Gwen said, *"I really feel like if he's willing to do the counseling with you there, that we should meet him in the middle."* I choked up because I knew she was right. I reluctantly muttered the words, *"OK, I'll do it."* But I wasn't happy about it at all!

TWO SIMPLE VERBS

While we were separated, Kevin ran into a young couple who had gone through some marital issues. When he mentioned that the two of us were not living together, they strongly recommended the book *Love and Respect* by Dr. Emerson Eggerichs, a marriage and family counselor. Later he spoke with his friend, John, who just so happened to recommend the *same* book. Thinking it too much of a coincidence, he relayed this information to Jerry, Gwen, and me. After looking into it, we discovered that the *Love and Respect* book came with a supplemental workbook and was ideal to use as the basis for counseling.

Dr. Eggerichs basically strips everything down to what he refers to as the Love and Respect Connection: that a woman's primary need is for *love* and a man's primary need is for *respect*. He believes that "Without love, she reacts without respect (toward him)", and "Without respect, he reacts without love (toward her)," which in turn causes a negative behavior pattern Eggerichs refers to as the Crazy Cycle. The basis for this principle is found in Ephesians 5:33

> However, each one of you also must **love his wife** as he loves himself, and the wife must **respect her husband.**

But how do you respect someone you feel is causing your deepest pain? And how does a man continue to love a woman who doesn't respect him? Those were the challenges we faced as we committed ourselves to working through our conflict with our counselors and our book.

I must admit, at first I was cynical.   After one chapter of Love and Respect, I told my pastor's wife that the book had better get better.   The case Dr. Eggerichs was making may have been true and relevant to us, but it didn't penetrate my jaded attitude. I'm sorry to admit that it was the first time in our relationship where I had little hope for the future. I was contemplating divorce.

Gradually, things did improve.   While going through the book with our counselors, Kevin and I gained a new awareness of how we had unconsciously been undermining each other's basic need. I realized that I could respect Kevin for who he was as a human being, created and loved by God—apart from anything he had done or not done.   Once Kevin felt this unconditional respect, he could in turn respond with unconditional love and affection for me.   It was a starting point.   By the time we were into the fourth chapter of Love and Respect as well as the fourth counseling session, we were becoming what I would call "cautious friends." We decided we would start dating!

We were like teenagers. Kevin would come and pick me up (or vice versa) and we would do the craziest things! We took long drives into sparsely traveled roads looking for wooded hiking trails to explore. We packed into to a crowded karaoke bar and Kevin sang a love song to me in front of everyone as I smiled awkwardly. Sometimes we would just sit on my back porch overlooking Mount Hood and watch the clouds and sunset. We even considered camping. (We never did appreciate hauling a bunch of camping equipment out to the boonies and then getting rained on or bitten by mosquitoes!)

I think the most important thing about this dating period is that we gave ourselves time to ignore the pressures of life for a while and just be friends again. We remembered how to have fun together!

The counseling continued to help Kevin and I uncover the layers that we had built up over the years through disappointments, false expectations, and unaccomplished dreams. There were many apologies, tears, and regrets. We each learned how to identify our triggers which had led to destructive defense mechanisms and negative behavior patterns (i.e., the before-mentioned crazy cycle!). Once we became aware of what caused these once knee-jerk reactions, we could apologize and begin to treat each other in a kinder manner. All in all, Kevin and I now have a much healthier relationship based on acting out these two simple verbs: love and respect.

Finally! After all these years, our foundation had become sturdy and strong! We could be a lighthouse, built on the Solid Rock, to shine as a beacon for others dealing with their own unique struggles. All because our loving Father's grace helps us turn our weak areas into strengths.

MORE THAN CONQUERORS

The year we overcame separation and divorce was the same year we celebrated our 30th wedding anniversary—the benchmark for us to get back together again. Together we can say, *"In all these things we are more than conquerors!"* Oh, if we only had known just how prophetic our marriage passage would be:

> **And we know that in all things God works for the good of those who love him, who have been called according to his purpose.** For those God foreknew he also predestined to be conformed to the likeness of his Son, that he might be the firstborn among many brothers. And to those he predestined, he also called; those he called, he also justified; those he justified, he also glorified.
>
> What, then, shall we say in response to this? **If God is for us, who can be against us?** He who did not spare his own Son, but gave him up for us all-how will he not also, along with him, graciously give us all things? Who will bring any charge against those whom God has chosen? It is God who justifies. Who is he that condemns? Christ Jesus, who died-more than that, who was raised to life-is at the right hand of God and is also interceding for us. **Who shall separate us from the love of Christ? Shall trouble or hardship or persecution or famine or nakedness or danger or sword?**

No, in all these things we are more than conquerors through him who loved us.

For I am convinced that neither death nor life, neither angels nor demons, neither the present nor the future, nor any powers, neither height nor depth, nor anything else in all creation, will be able to separate us from the love of God that is in Christ Jesus our Lord. (Romans 8:28-35, 37-39 NIV, emphasis added.)

The road of life is not a direct line from A to B, but it is instead a road full of twists and turns, unexpected potholes, long monotonous stretches of highway, and even detours. We don't have a digital navigation system for life into which we simply plug a destination, in order to receive the "shortest and easiest route," one that avoids all obstacles, delays, and road closures. Instead, in the path of life, there should be a sign that reads, **"Trouble and Hardship Ahead, Plan for Delays."** I like what Dave Roever, the once critically wounded veteran soldier, says, "You don't have to go looking for trouble, it will find you!"

When I was a young girl, my brothers and I had a toy that I will never forget called Bobo the Clown Bop Bag. It was a three-and-a-half foot tall bowling-pin shaped latex clown filled with air that had a couple inches of sand on the bottom to keep it upright. The goal, of course, was to punch it hard enough to keep it down…only it never stayed down, unless my brothers and I would sit on it! Bobo would simply take the hit, and then slowly bop back up!

Our lives are like that bop bag and the love of Christ is like the sand on the bottom. The trials of life are constantly throwing punches at us. These punches come in many forms. Sometimes we find ourselves in a fight because of our own bad choices and we get beaten up. At other times, we have been blindsided when a punch hits us square in the face and completely knocks the course of our life sideways. And still at other times, a destructive life pattern of ours or a loved one keeps knocking us down over and over again. There may even come a point where we feel so much shame and defeat we just want to stay down on the floor because we've lost hope of ever getting back up again.

When we put our faith in Christ who lives in us, how can we possibly stay down? Even if it takes endurance and a lot of suffering on our part, His love will *always* cause us to rise back up again. In fact, after all the defeats we've had in life, isn't it amazing that He refers to His people as conquerors? And He says we are not just conquerors—we are MORE than conquerors!!! Why? Inside those of us who have accepted Christ is the spirit of a conqueror! And that Conqueror has overcome death, hell, and the grave! Christ Jesus fought the fiercest battle of all when He gave up His life to die on a cross for our sins. And fortunately for us, He won that battle against the warrior of evil, the devil, when *He rose* from death to life eternal. He got back up!

In the movie *The Last Samurai* to which I referred in the fourth section of this book, the protagonist had sustained many severe blows before he was lying wounded on his back in the pouring rain. But if you continue to watch the movie, Nathan eventually gets up. And the story doesn't stop there. Over the course of time, he learns how to fight as a samurai warrior. He develops a deep affinity with the tribe. He becomes a fierce swordsman and wins the Samurai people's love and respect.

Nelson Mandela has a wonderful quote. *"Don't judge me by successes, but how many times I fell down and got back up again."* Kevin and I had to decide that we would not allow shame from past mistakes to paralyze us and keep us from a productive future. According to the passage in Romans, no matter what we go through—trouble, hardship, shame, danger or war—it will never separate us from the love of Christ or the love we have for each other. We can entrust everything in our lives that's ever knocked us down to our Mighty Champion who can take what the enemy caused for evil and turn it into something good. That's true redemption!

OUR PURPOSE UNVEILED

I'm pretty sure everyone has done something stupid that caused them to ask the question, *"What was I thinking?"* While Kevin was in prison, he embarked on a journey of self-reflection that caused him to ask this probing question as well as an even deeper question, *"Why* was I thinking that?" Furthermore, he began to ask himself, *"If I was so duped by Lawrence, what other beliefs did I hold that might be just as wrong?"* In finding the answers to these questions he studied concepts like worldview, presuppositions, biases and values. He learned how to challenge his own thinking to create a new mindset. He discovered that changing your thinking results in changing your behavior, and that changing your behavior will ultimately change the course of your life.

After Kevin was released from prison, a friend asked him, *"What was the biggest lesson you learned in prison?"* He thought about it a moment and then replied, *"Blind spots! We all have them."* This one realization birthed in him a passion to discover psychological blind spots and then help others recognize and mitigate the blind spots that skew and influence their decision-making abilities.

In 2016, Kevin launched a professional speaking and coaching career, leveraging his prison story along with the many lessons he learned and wrote about in his book entitled *Blind Spots—Why Good People Make Bad Choices*. Kevin's mission is ultimately to empower business leaders and organizations, so they can make better decisions in the workplace, in their personal life, and in all areas of influence.

After more than twenty-five years of working with children, in the fall of 2017, I completely changed my career path to serve alongside Kevin in his company, assisting with writing materials, book sales, and best of all, travel. I became his constant companion, flying all over the nation, to various corporate audiences who seek to hear his unique prison story and the lessons therein. I have stood behind many book tables at the end of speaking events as attendees come to ask me the prevailing question, *"How did you do it?"*

This prompted my decision in the spring of 2018 to begin telling my side of the story. I was inspired to share a message of hope and redemption in the face of adversity in the book you are now reading. My desire was (and is) not only to publish this book, but also to reach predominantly female audiences to help empower and equip women to overcome adversity. But once again, moving forward would not be easy.

ROAD BLOCKS

Shortly after gathering information on the process of writing a book and sharing the decision to write my story with friends and family, I hit not one, but two road blocks.

Ironically, the week before Mother's Day 2018, I received some alarming news from my gynecologist that they had found a "suspicious area" on my mammogram. Being an optimist, I didn't give the suspicion any credence, but still went through with my doctors' orders to have a special imaging clinic obtain a closer look, with the mindset that I would get a clean bill of health and move on with my life and my book.

After the specialized mammogram, the technician sent me to another room for an ultrasound. Surprisingly, the ultrasound revealed a small, nebulous, dark area which the sweet, gray-haired female doctor claimed would need a biopsy.

I was still in a state of optimism and disbelief when the same lovely doctor did the biopsy the following week. After seeing the mysterious black spot with my own eyes on the screen beside me, I naively asked the doctor, *"So will this need to be removed if it's only a cyst?"*

The doctor was quiet. That's when I realized I had asked the wrong question. So I rephrased it, *"So, do you actually think it's cancer?"* The doctor hesitated and then said gently, *"Yes, I'm sorry to say, it is. I've seen thousands of these and the tumor has the same tell-tale signs. But we'll know something more when we receive the results from the lab in a couple days."* I don't remember at that point what I said, but I'm pretty sure my mouth was hanging open. I was truly in shock!

The doctor had recommended that Kevin come with me for the biopsy, so he was waiting in the lobby. The attendant guided the two of us into a little room with pink pillows on the chairs, free pink puffy pens and a container of pink rubber bracelets with the inscribed phrase "I BEAT CANCER." We both sat there in amazement as I heard the word *cancer* come out of my own mouth.

Later, as we drove home with the awful news weighing heavily on our minds, I looked at Kevin and said, *"Wow, I was in such a happy place!"* I realized that I had *finally* come to a place of peace in so many areas of my life. Peace in my home, peace in my marriage, peace in my heart, and peace with my health. I was just really happy! I took pride in the fact that when the receptionist had given me the sheet with the mental health questionnaire regarding depression, anxiety, anger, and suicidal thoughts, I was able to check the NO box for all of them! And now here I was with breast cancer!? Kevin glanced over at me as he drove and said, *"Stay in your happy place!"* *"Well, that is exactly what I'm going to do,"* I said, *"And I am not going to let this affect me!"* Two days later I received the impending phone call: *Ductal Carcinoma In Situ, Stage One.*

Still reeling from the first road block, I came upon another. A little over a month later, and a few chapters into writing my book, Kevin and I traveled to Missoula, Montana, where he was scheduled to do a keynote for a CPA conference. After we checked into our hotel and had a bite to eat, we rented a couple of bikes to explore our beautiful, small-town surroundings. At the end of the day, we came back to our hotel to shower and prepare for the conference the next morning.

When I stepped into the shower, it felt as if my foot hit a sheet of glass on an icy road. Suddenly, both feet went out from under me and I had nothing to grab onto! My body fell like a tower over the side of the tub and I crashed head first into the back of the toilet stool, slicing my forehead from above my eyebrow to below my eyelid. Pain exploded through my face and head as I screamed for Kevin, who came running from the other room. Blood started to drip heavily into the tub and all around me as I squatted down in horror. Kevin acted fast when he saw the gash. He quickly grabbed a hand towel and had me hold it tightly up against the wound while he ran to call 911.

Thank goodness for small towns! In less than thirty minutes, I was lying on my back in the emergency room accompanied by nurses and a doctor. Unfortunately, my brain tissue swelled from the impact, pressing against the skull causing excruciating pain that not even the Fentanyl in the IV could match. But even that pain was nothing compared to the shots of Lidocaine the doctor administered directly into the laceration across my orbital bone in order to numb the severed skin. While he was doing his careful stitching, tears rolled down my unmoving cheeks. When the nurse asked me about my medical history and came to the question about cancer, I cried like a baby.

Never, did I think I would answer "YES" to this question. Especially now!

These two experiences and the accompanying physical and psychological pain really threw me for a loop. With my head still throbbing, a barrage of ongoing appointments with oncologists, and nonstop phone calls with insurance personnel, I painfully tried to make sense of it all.

Again, I directed my cries toward heaven, *"God, what is going on? I thought you were my shield and protection?! What is this all about?"* The truth be told, I really felt abandoned by Him, almost like He had stepped away for a while and just let me get beat up. This time, my symbolic Bobo was not bouncing back as quickly as it used to. I couldn't move forward with anything! The doctor had ordered me to stay off all technology while my brain healed. (I actually found out thinking is a physical exercise and blue light makes it worse.) I couldn't write, I wasn't any help to Kevin, and I couldn't even do simple tasks like gardening for more than two hours without my head hurting. My life was at a standstill.

About the time the majority of the pain in my head subsided, I had the scheduled five-hour surgery to remove the cancer and do the reduction-lift that is not uncommon after breast tissue removal. (I don't know any woman that prefers to be lopsided!) I came home from the hospital looking like I had been chopped in half, and then stitched from one side to the other. But the pain and accompanying scars were overshadowed by good news! The tissue samples they sent to the lab came back negative. *Hallelujah! No more cancer!* Just a big, ugly scar left in the wake of an ominous black tumor.

In order for me to stay in my happy place during all of this, I had to keep the clichéd "attitude of gratitude." The fall and resulting concussion could have been *so much worse!* Yes, I do have a nasty scar and some nerve damage, but I could've lost my right eye, had brain damage (some may think I do anyway!), or memory loss. As far as the cancer is concerned, the tumor was discovered at an early stage! It had not metastasized and there were no cancer cells found in my lymph system. I did not need chemotherapy which meant I got to keep my hair and eyebrows. I had many reasons to be thankful!

GRIT AND VULNERABILITY

One early morning shortly after the surgery, I was in my office asking God what He was teaching me through all of this. I wanted to glean all the gems I could from this grueling six months. As I was praying, I received a mental picture of what I call *"The Parable of the Two Sailors."* It goes like this:

There were two sailors standing side by side. Each of them was captain of his own fishing vessel which they chartered on the open, sometimes dangerous, sea. Both had a captain's license. My job was to interview each of them and decide who I trusted the most to take me aboard his boat to sail out into the deep ocean.

The first sailor was well-dressed in his pressed, white uniform, clean-shaven and very well put together. His boat looked somewhat new and hardly broken in. The second sailor was burly, tattooed, had a couple scars, and when he spoke, let's just say, he used some colorful language. His boat was weathered and worn, although it was still very sea-worthy.

Now the question came to me, *"Which sailor am I going to trust?"* The one who looked like he was fresh out of Sailor School and taking his boat out for the first time, or the sailor who had weathered some serious squalls, learned how to navigate treacherous waters, and had the scars and stories to prove it? Well, the answer is obvious. I'm going with the one who's got GRIT!

And so it is with me! I realized I needed to be "Gritty, not pretty!" I gotta have some scars that tell of the storms I've encountered in the "waters" of life. And I need to have the courage to point my ship's bow directly into the fury of life and face reality, good, bad or otherwise, knowing that God *is* with me, even when the sky is dark and the waves are fierce! My faith must be strong enough to believe that He who made the seas with a whisper is aboard my ship and He will guide me safely to the shore!

The definition of grit according to Merriam Webster's dictionary is *"Firmness of mind or spirit: unyielding courage in the face of hardship or danger."* Wow! I want to emulate this kind of character. I'm praying God will help me "turn my fear into fierce and my gutless into grit." I printed these words out in a large font, and hung them on my office wall. Grit is something I had been lacking! Now I just need a nice big tattoo across my chest! (Haha, maybe not!)

The other gem I discovered while my life was on hold is just how much we *need* each other. To admit you need someone is to let down your wall of self-sufficiency and become *vulnerable*. Practically, it is to admit you can't do something alone and you're going to need help. I realize the words grit and vulnerability sound like they're contradictory, but actually they work perfectly together! As renowned psychologist Brené Brown states, "Vulnerability is not weakness, it's our greatest measure of courage."

For me, this vulnerability did not come easily. I really had to humble myself and allow the weakness of my injuries, as well as those around me, including Kevin, my parents, and my friends, to penetrate my self-reliance.

Kevin was my rock star as I went through the cancer surgery, concussion, and recovery from both. He was there to help me when I was bedridden and never once begrudged it. With each incident, he kept a chart of all my meds, making sure I got the right dose at the right time, even when it required getting up in the middle of the night. (You understand the importance of this if you or a loved one has had a serious illness or injury.)

At one of my follow-up appointments, I was talking to a nurse about Kevin being on one of his business trips and her response shocked me. She said, *"Ah, whatever. We don't need them."* Without sounding combative, I replied, *"Oh man, I do need my husband. I can't imagine going through all this without him!"* My guess is that she hadn't had a situation yet that had forced her into a position of vulnerability.

We're living in a culture where women are realizing their strength and fierce independence more and more. Though I'm not saying that is a bad thing, I would add that when men and women are *interdependent*, they are even stronger than they are individually.

The Bible declares in Ecclesiastes 4:9-12:

> Two people are better off than one, for they can help each other succeed. If one person falls, the other can reach out and help. But someone who falls alone is in real trouble. Likewise, two people lying close together can keep each other warm. But how can one be warm alone? A person standing alone can be attacked and defeated, but two can stand back-to-back and conquer. Three are even better, for a triple-braided cord is not easily broken. (New Living Translation)

The verse I'd like to emphasize in this passage is twelve: *"A person standing alone can be attacked and defeated, but two can stand back-to-back and conquer!"* Even when we are wearing the full armor of God, there is nothing that covers our backside. As Kevin teaches in his seminars, we are unaware of our blind spots. This is why we need our life partners and friends! When we have each other's back, our success multiplies. And best of all, we enjoy the sweetness of victory, or in my case, the sweetness of *healing*, together!

REFLECTIONS

Last August, Kevin and I celebrated our thirty-second wedding anniversary! Having feelings of regret about being party to the HMC/Znetix scandal and the resulting incarceration would be unproductive. Reflection, on the other hand, is good, especially when we can reflect upon our lives and see how our past so wonderfully aligns with the purpose for our future.

Had none of this narrative ever happened, I would never have become so trusting in a God who so faithfully cared for me in every way during a time of such great need. The adversity I experienced over many years became to me the finest school of learning I could have ever been through; taught by the very Master Himself. Once again I look to L.B. Cowman's words of wisdom, *"The school of suffering graduates exceptional scholars."*

And Kevin, had he never gone to Sheridan for thirty-three months, would never have explored the deep questions of life resulting in a very eye-opening and intriguing dissertation and book. Out of our rubble has come a story of redemption we can share with the world!

And oh, how grateful we are now. We are grateful for each other, that we would not allow the circumstances we faced to tear us apart. When Kevin was incarcerated, I was grateful for his encouraging love letters. I'm grateful that through it all, he didn't give up on himself. I'm grateful he didn't lose hope for the future. And most importantly, he didn't give up on God!

Kevin is grateful too. He is grateful I didn't abandon him and that I didn't give up on him. He knows that I continued to believe in him!!! He is a good man, and becoming a better one, day by day.

In his presentations, Kevin always refers to me as the hero of the story (or the shero as I call it.) But in actuality, God stands far above all else as The Hero! He helped Kevin and me remain steadfast in our relationship to Him, and to each other. He filled us with hope to carry on. In my weakest moments, I know He lifted me up and carried me, and when Kevin couldn't take anymore, He carried him. It was His relentless love and grace that enabled the two of us to cross the finish line—together!

I will end this story with one final letter from a prisoner, now free. Kevin didn't realize when he put his pen to his notebook paper so many years ago just how potent these words would be in our lives. I treasure these words dearly and hope that someday I will live up to them:

10/23/5

Hi Rach,

Thanks for spending so much time with me today. I really enjoyed our heart-to-heart talks. God is at work in both of us. Keep seeking him and everything will be added to you. He has big plans for you. Remember all your dreams and aspirations you had when we first met. He is bringing us back to a new start.

You've been faithful and are well-pleasing to Him. All of the lessons you have learned and are now learning will be used to bring significant change and hope to God's people. You'll be able to speak with authority and conviction, with speech full of compassion. Your words will be like medicine to many wounded souls. So, remember all the observations you are making, the feelings you are having, the victories you are receiving.

I'm proud of you, my champion. This is the hardest thing you've had to endure. You are pulling through better then you probably realize. You are strong and getting stronger. Remember, not our will but HIS WILL BE DONE. To Him be the glory, forever!

I love you—Kevin

Conclusion

The number one question I get, mostly from other women is, how was I able to forgive Kevin for what he put us through? As a colleague put it, "He went to prison, but I did the real time."

I cannot answer that question without first saying that I have come to know that God is a gracious and compassionate God, who desires to forgive the sins of those who acknowledge His Son Jesus and the sacrifice He made for all men to be forgiven. The Bible tells us in Rom 3:22-25:

> This righteousness from God comes through
> faith in Jesus Christ to all who believe. There is
> no difference, for all have sinned and fall short of
> the glory of God, and are justified freely by his
> grace through the redemption that came by
> Christ Jesus. God presented him as a sacrifice of
> atonement, through faith in his blood.

This passage levels the playing field. We *all* have sinned. In other words, not one of us is more righteous than another. Only God could make us right in His sight by sending His one and only Son Jesus to suffer, die in our place, and free us from the penalty of our sins. It is only when we believe that Jesus shed his own blood for us that we can receive *redemption* from all of our sins.

Here is the same concept in the Old Testament book of Isaiah:

> But he was pierced for our transgressions, he was crushed for our iniquities; the punishment that brought us peace was upon him, and by his wounds we are healed. We **all,** like sheep, have gone astray, **each of us** has turned to his own way; and the LORD has laid on him the iniquity of us all. (53:5-6 NIV)

We *all* (there is that word *all* again) have gone astray. *Each one of us* has gone his own way.

We were all guilty of prison, and even worse, eternal damnation. But because the Lord loved us so, He sent His Son to take the punishment for all of us.

Having said this, my answer to that familiar question is, "Because I knew that I too, had been forgiven, how could I not also freely forgive?"

Jesus told his disciples in Matthew 6:14-15:

> For if you forgive men when they sin against you, your heavenly Father will also forgive you. But if you do not forgive men their sins, your Father will not forgive your sins. (NIV)

Christ gave Himself up for us. So we ought to give ourselves up for one another. We can only love (and forgive) because he first loved (and forgave) us. If we are going to follow Christ and walk as He walked, then forgiveness is a requirement. God wants the best for us. He knows that when we hold something against someone, it puts us in an emotional state of bondage. Psychologists seem to agree that unforgiveness and bitterness are damaging to our mental health as well as our physical health. Over time, the negative thoughts and emotions we hold on to take a toll on our bodies. We can't truly be happy, healthy, and whole until we let go and forgive those who have hurt us.

Now I would be lying if I told you that forgiving Kevin was easy. I constantly had to rely on God's grace working through me to love and forgive him. It wasn't something that happened overnight, but instead, it was a process. I continually had to let go of my feelings of grief, anger, and resentment, and ask God to give me His heart of mercy and forgiveness. Often times, there is a wrestling in our hearts before we completely submit to His will. But doing so gives us tremendous peace.

Secondly, I also had to remember that I needed to forgive him regardless of whether he *deserved* my forgiveness or not. Forgiving him had to be an act of my will and not an emotion that I would feel. I had to "set my will" to forgive at all times. Once we make the decision that we *are* going to forgive no matter what offenses come our way, forgiveness seems to come easier than if we wait till the anger of the moment.

So, the ultimate answer to the question of *"How did you do it?"*

Without Christ and His empowerment, I would have never made it through this battlefield. I would've

145

been another casualty of war and statistic for divorce. But instead, I can say:

> …but thanks be to God, who gives us the victory through our Lord Jesus Christ. Therefore, my beloved brethren, be steadfast, immovable, always abounding in the work of the Lord, knowing that your toil is not in vain in the Lord. (1 Corinthians 15:57-58 NASB)

My final words to you are these:

> This is real love—not that we loved God, but that he loved us and sent his Son as a sacrifice to take away our sins. Dear friends, since God so loved us that much, we surely ought to love each other. No one has ever seen God; but if we love each other, God lives in us, and his love is brought to full expression in us. (1 John 4:10-12 NLT)

Works Cited

L.B. Cowman, Streams in the Desert Morning and Evening: 365 Devotions (Zondervan, November 1, 2016).

Annie Johnson Flint, "He Givith More Grace," Timeless Truths Free Online Library, https://library.timelesstruths.org/music/He_Giveth_More_Grace/.

Emerson Eggerichs, Love & Respect Study Set - Love & Respect: The Love She Most Desires, the Respect He Desperately Needs (Book + Workbook), (Thomas Nelson; 2005).

Dave Roever, message to Horizon Community Church Tualatin, Oregon 2018

Goodreads, Nelson Mandela > Quotes > Quotable Quote, https://www.goodreads.com/quotes/270163-do-not-judge-me-by-my-successes-judge-me-by.

Kevin McCarthy, Blind Spots: Why Good People Make Bad Choices (Healy Quinn Publishers, First edition, July 19, 2017).

Merriam-Webster's Collegiate Dictionary. 11th ed. Springfield, MA: Merriam-Webster, 2008. Continually updated at https://www.merriam-webster.com/.

Goodreads, Rising Strong Quotes, Brené Brown, https://www.goodreads.com/work/quotes/42872911-rising-strong.

The Harness of the Lord—A prophetic revelation, received and recorded by Bill Britton (1918-1985) in the 1960's. The Open Scroll at https://www.theopenscroll.com/hosting/TheHarnessOfTheLord_BillBritton.htm

For bulk orders of this book or to inquire about speaking availability for your next conference or corporate event, church service, women's group or retreat, contact me directly.

Rachel Joy McCarthy

+1-503-770-0036

+1-877-527-9613

Connect with the author at:

Website: www.LettersFromaPrisoner.com

LinkedIn: www.LinkedIn.com/in/RJoyMcCarthy

Twitter: www.Twitter.com/RJoyMcCarthy

https://www.facebook.com/RJoyMcCarthy

https://www.instagram.com/RJoyMcCarthy

40153334R00094

Made in the USA
Middletown, DE
24 March 2019